THE BLACK CROWES
GUITAR ANTHOLOGY SERIES

CONTENTS

Transcribed by DANNY BEGELMAN

Project Manager: AARON STANG
Assistant Editor: COLGAN BRYAN
Cover Design: JOSEPH KLUCAR
Book Art Layout: RAFAEL D' SABINO

<u>Cover Art</u>

Shake Your Money Maker
© 1990 Def American Recordings, Inc.

The Southern Harmony and Music Companion
© 1992 Def American Recordings, Inc.

Amorica
© 1994 American Recordings

Three Snakes and One Charm
© 1996 American Recordings

By Your Side
© 1998 Sony Music Entertainment Inc.

WARNER BROS. PUBLICATIONS - THE GLOBAL LEADER IN PRINT
USA: 15800 NW 48th Avenue, Miami, FL 33014

 WARNER/CHAPPELL MUSIC

 Carisch NUOVA CARISCH

 IMP INTERNATIONAL MUSIC PUBLICATIONS LIMITED

CANADA: 40 SHEPPARD AVE. WEST, SUITE 800
TORONTO, ONTARIO, M2N 6K9
SCANDINAVIA: P.O. BOX 533, VENDEVAGEN 85 B
S-182 15, DANDERYD, SWEDEN
AUSTRALIA: P.O. BOX 353
3 TALAVERA ROAD, NORTH RYDE N.S.W. 2113

ITALY: VIA CAMPANIA, 12
20098 S. GIULIANO MILANESE (MI)
ZONA INDUSTRIALE SESTO ULTERIANO
SPAIN: MAGALLANES, 25
28015 MADRID
FRANCE: 20, RUE DE LA VILLE-L'EVEQUE, 75008 PARIS

ENGLAND: GRIFFIN HOUSE,
161 HAMMERSMITH ROAD, LONDON W6 8BS
GERMANY: MARSTALLSTR. 8, D-80539 MUNCHEN
DENMARK: DANMUSIK, VOGNMAGERGADE 7
DK 1120 KOBENHAVNK

A CONSPIRACY

Words and Music by
CHRIS ROBINSON and
RICH ROBINSON

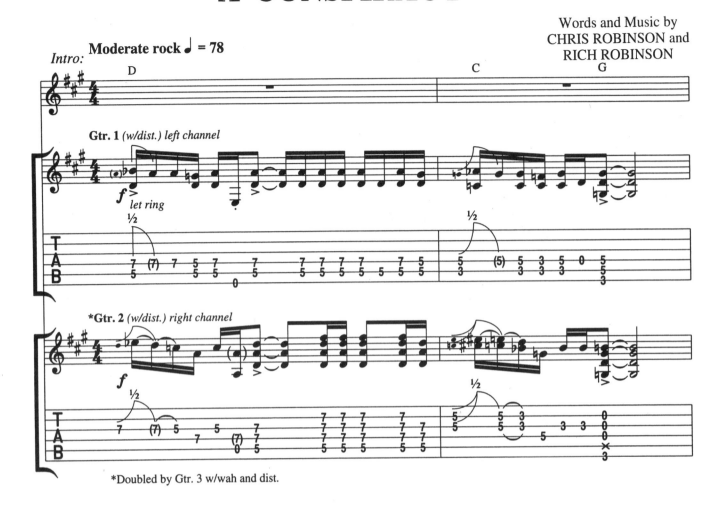

*Doubled by Gtr. 3 w/wah and dist.

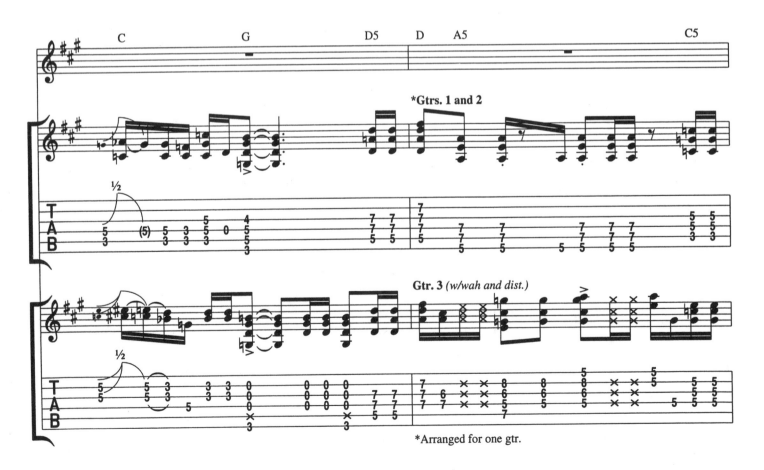

*Arranged for one gtr.

4

a - bout last year. ___ Said, it was all a lie. _____ Ain't it fun-ny how

time flies. Said, what we gon-na do, ba - by?_____ What's

end Rhy. Fig. 1

8

9

*Play on *D.S.*

*Doubled by Gtr. 3

A Conspiracy – 11 – 8

10

Organem Solo:

Yeah.

Verse 2:
So, now you got a question,
About your answer, yeah, yeah, yeah.
I try your Adam's apple,
Oh, you talk it, try it, like it, right.
Say, do you wanna fight?
Well, alright, say, let's step outside.
I got tradition, it's an addition.
My definition, it don't hold me back.
Well, what you think about that?
What you don't understand,
This is a very old land.

HARD TO HANDLE

Words and Music by
OTIS REDDING, ALVERTIS ISBELL
and ALLEN JONES

Hard to Handle - 9 - 1

14

I've got some good old lov-in' and I got some more in store. Uh,

when I get through throw-in' it on ya, you got to come back for more. (end Rhy. Fig. 1)

Chorus

Boys have things that come by the doz-en. That ain't noth-in' but drug-store lov-in'.

Pret-ty lit-tle thing, let me light your can-dle 'cause, uh, ma-ma, I'm sure hard to han-dle now, yes, a-round.

prove ev'-ry word I say.___ I'm_ ad -ver-tis - in' love_ for free, so you can

place your ad with me._____ Boys that come a -long, a dime_ by the doz-en.

That ain't noth -in' but ten cent lov -in'.

Pret -ty lit -tle thing let me light your can-dle 'cause, uh, ma - ma, I'm sure hard to han-dle now, yes, a -round.

18

20

DOWNTOWN MONEY WASTER

Gtrs. 1 and 2 in G tuning:
⑥ = D ③ = G
⑤ = G ② = B
④ = D ① = D

Intro:

Freely

Gtr. 1 *(Acoustic dobro) dbld. by mandolin*

Words and Music by
CHRIS ROBINSON and
RICH ROBINSON

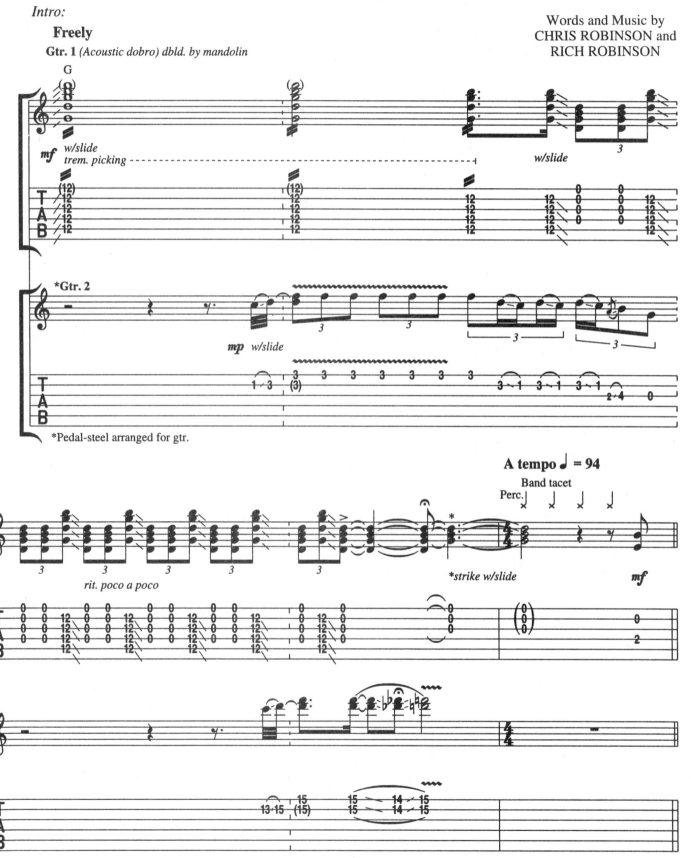

*Pedal-steel arranged for gtr.

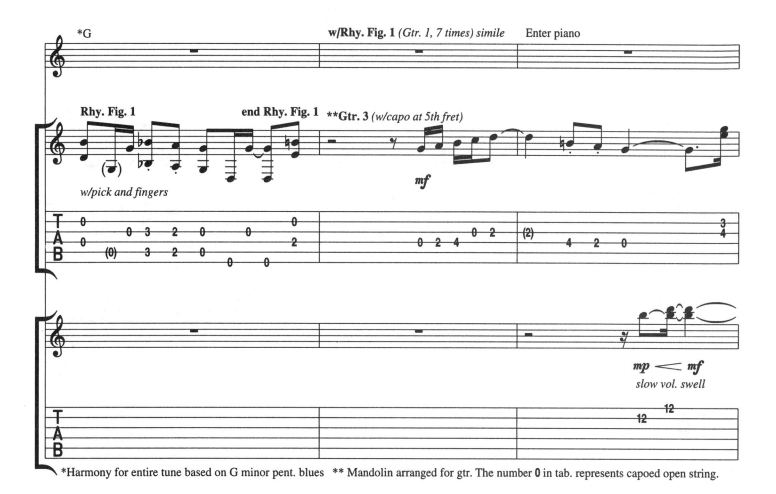

*Harmony for entire tune based on G minor pent. blues   ** Mandolin arranged for gtr. The number **0** in tab. represents capoed open string.

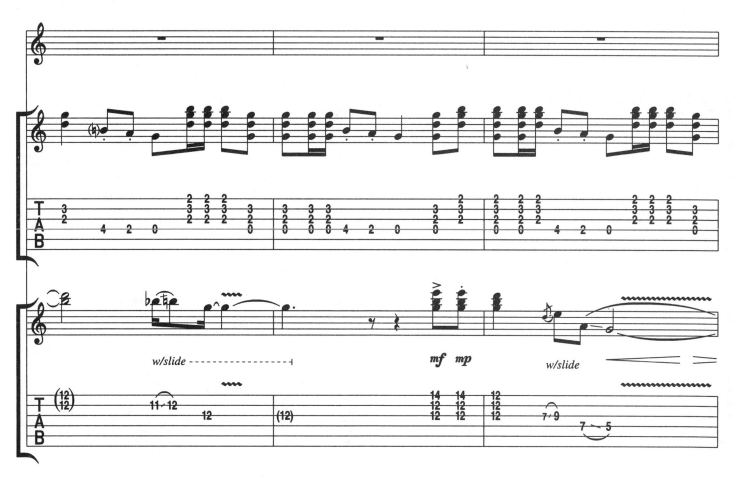

Verse:

w/Rhy. Fig. 1 *(Gtr. 1, 9 times) simile*

1. Low _____ down _

_____ down - town mon - ey wast - er. Well _____ you're sav -

2. *See additional lyrics*

in' grace _____ is that I liked to taste you but your flow - er is

Gtr. 2

Chorus:

end Rhy. Fig. 2

1.

28

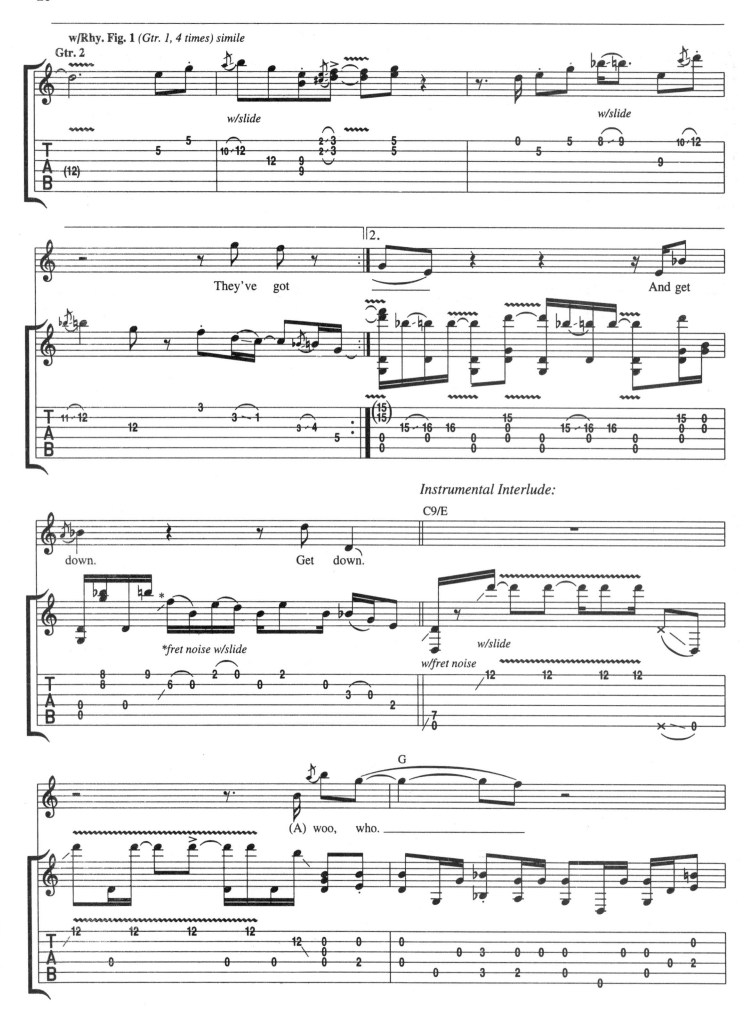

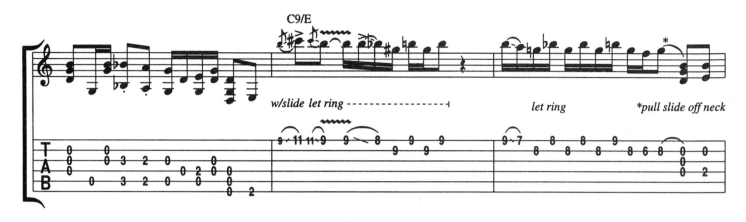

w/Rhy. Fig. 1 *(Gtr. 1, 6 times) simile*

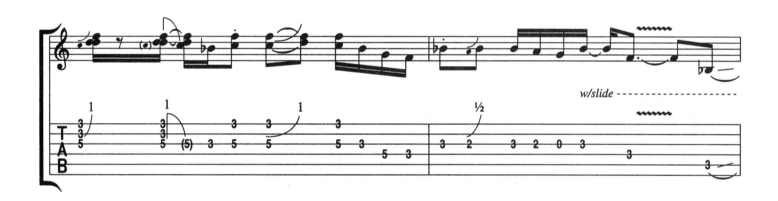

Verse:
w/Rhy. Fig. 1 *(Gtr. 1, 4 times) simile*

3. To my low ___ down ___ down - town ___

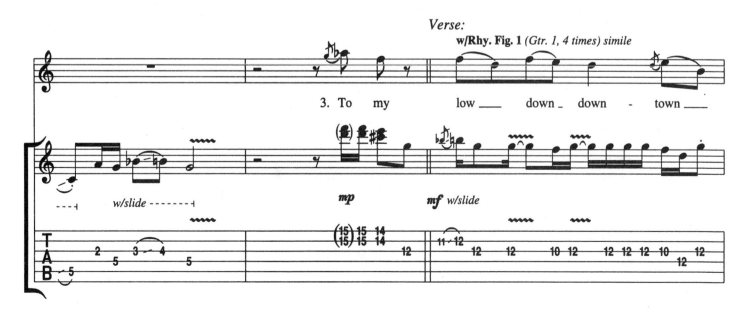

31

Verse 2:
(They got) two for one at the store on the corner,
Little girl like to drink and sniffin' powders.
Like the bars that stay open after hours,
Like the boys that go 24-7.
Too many late nights and you don't go to heaven.

Downtown Money Waster – 10 – 10

GOOD FRIDAY

Words and Music by
CHRISTOPHER ROBINSON
and RICH ROBINSON

Slow rock ♩ = 62

Intro:

*Gtr. 2: ① = D.
Gtr. 2 is elec. gtr. and pedal steel gtr. arr. for one.

Verse:

1. We've been a-void-ing this ___ for ___ so long. ___

w/Rhy. Fig. 1 *(Gtr. 1) 4 times, simile*

Lux - u-ry ___ is tem - po - rar - y, then ___ it's gone.

Good Friday – 6 – 2

34

Good Friday – 6 – 3

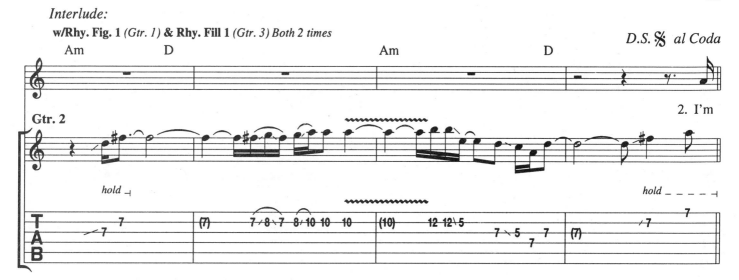

Good Friday – 6 – 4

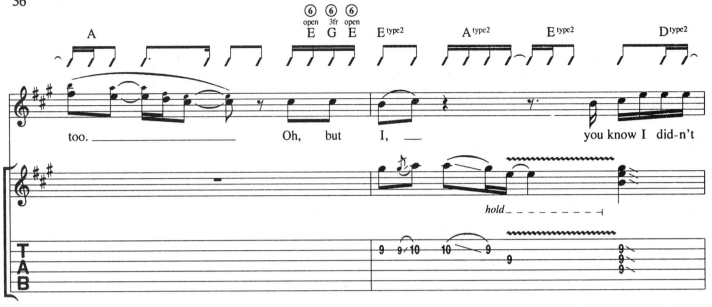

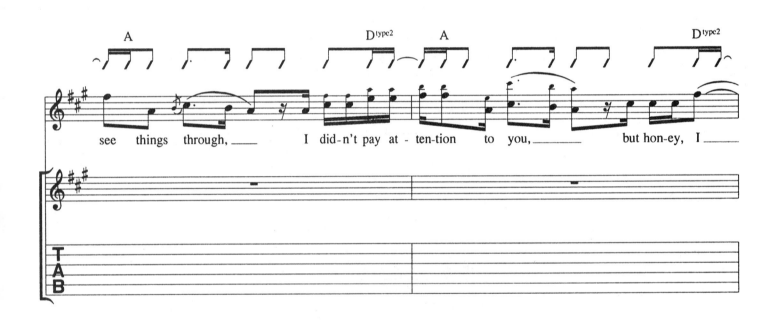

Verse 2:
I'm sorry I couldn't do this yesterday.
Tomorrow I am busy and what it is I can't say.
And Saturday is no good,
We've got a show.
So it has to be Good Friday,
Then it's so long.
(To Chorus:)

GONE

Words and Music by
CHRIS ROBINSON and
RICH ROBINSON

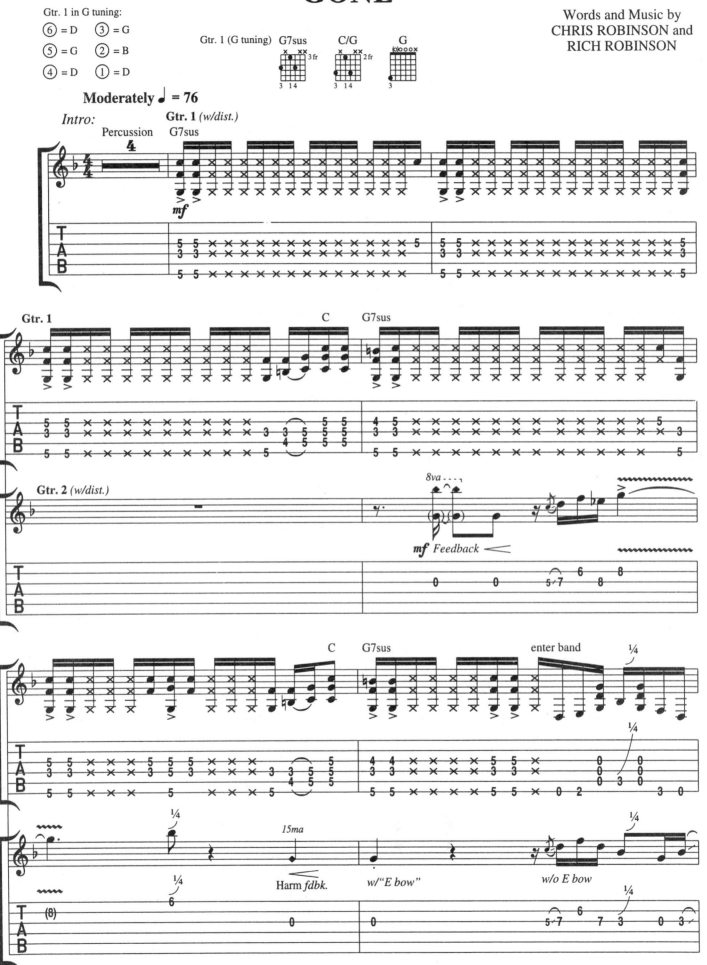

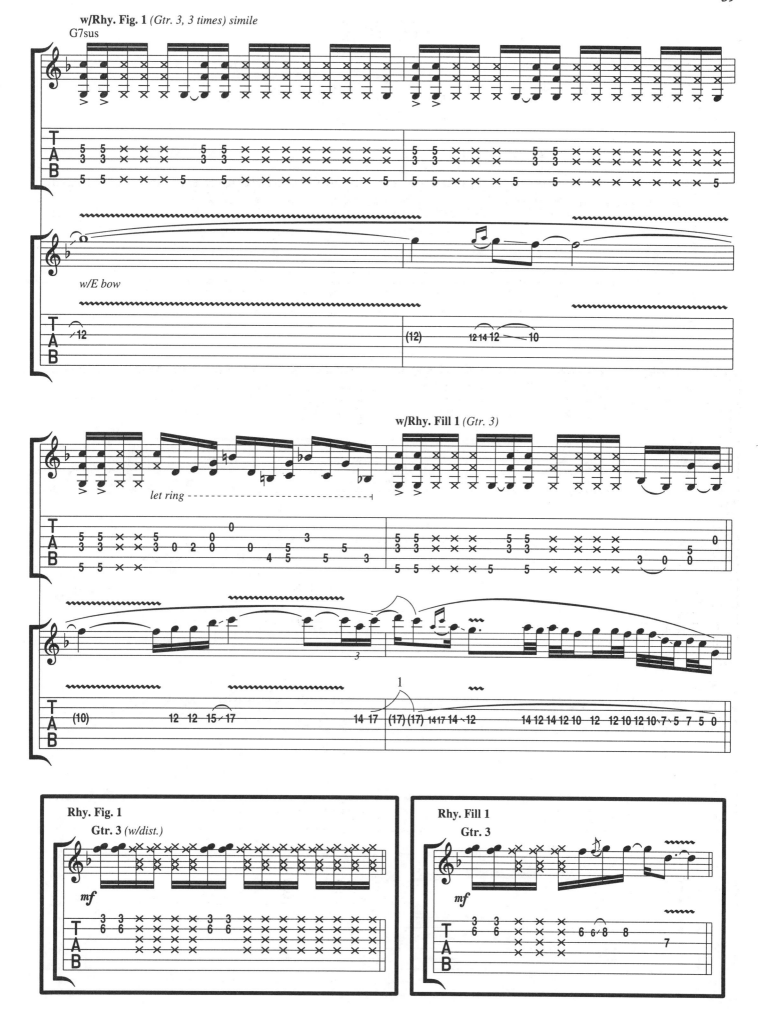

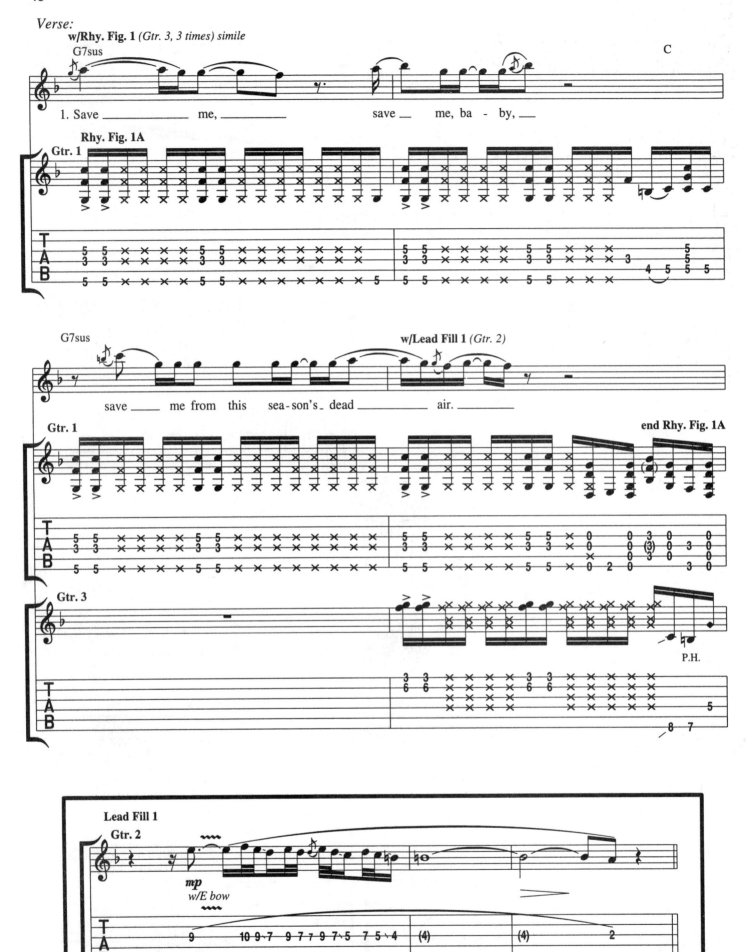

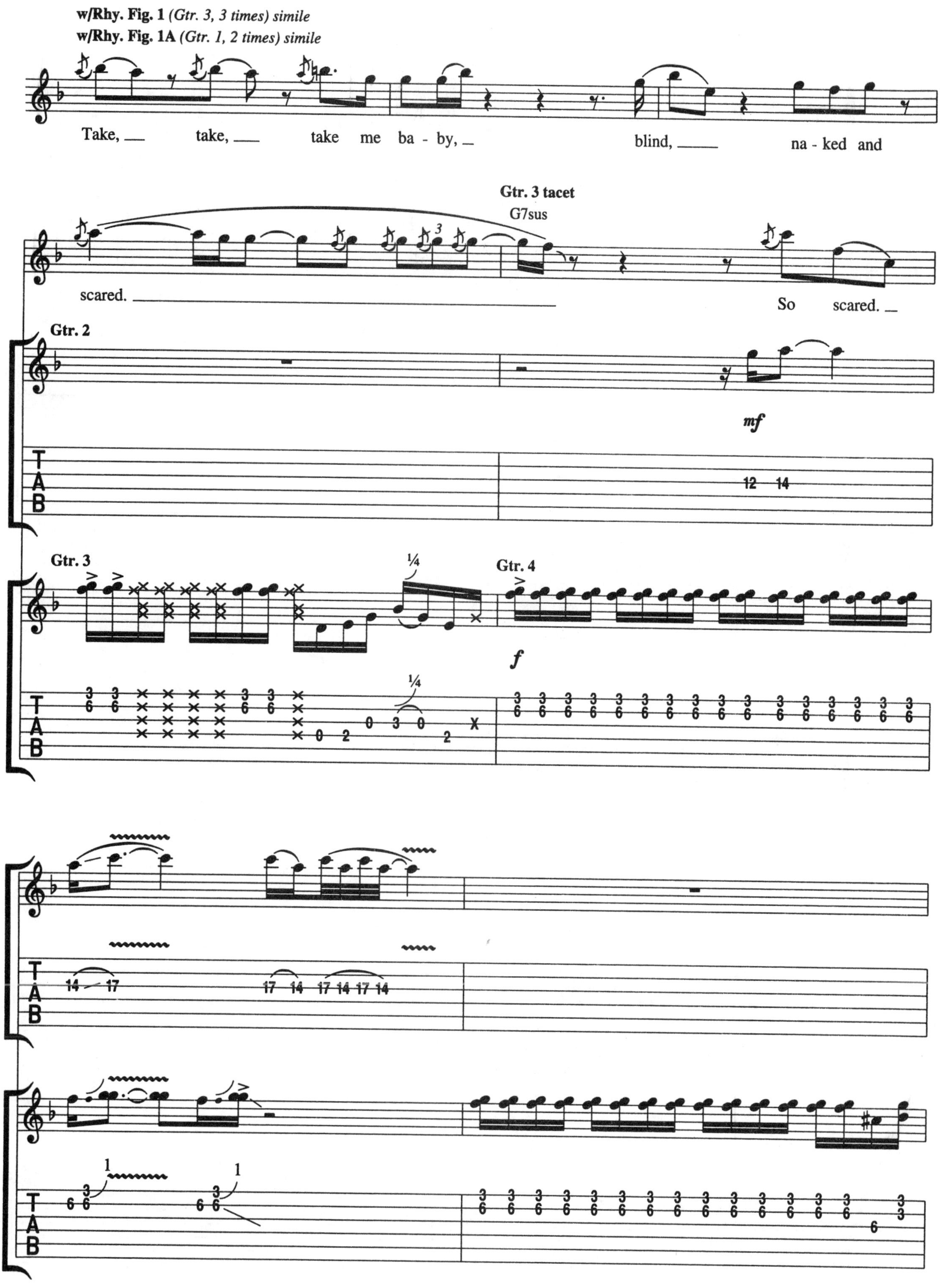

w/Rhy. Fig. 1 (Gtr. 3, 3 times) simile
w/Rhy. Fig. 1A (Gtr. 1, 2 times) simile
Take, take, take me ba - by, blind, na - ked and
Gtr. 3 tacet
G7sus
scared. So scared.
Gtr. 2
mf
Gtr. 3
Gtr. 4
f

42

Verse:
w/Rhy. Fig. 1 *(Gtr. 3, 3 times) simile*
w/Rhy. Fig. 1A *(Gtr. 1, 2 times) simile*

2. Want you to burn _____ me, _____ burn _____ me, _

4. *See additional lyrics*

Gtr. 2 *on D.S.*

mp

____ ba - by. ___ Burn me ___ and cov - er your eyes _ with my

ash - es. ____   Come on __ and why don't you pray _____ for me,

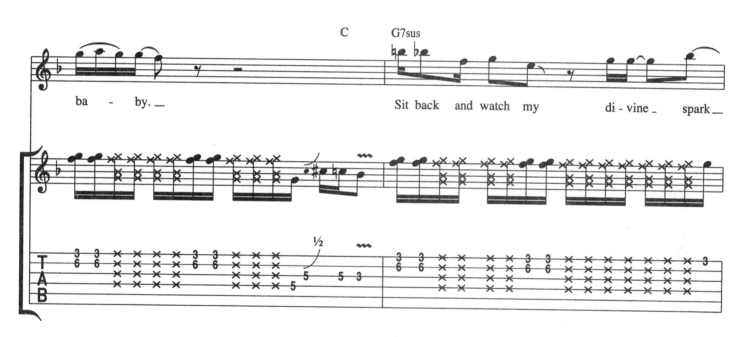

ba - by. __   Sit back and watch my di - vine __ spark __

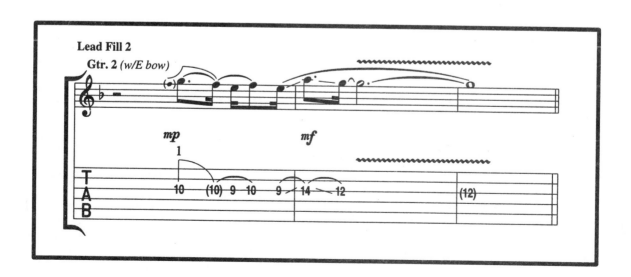

*E locrian tonality throughout this measure.

46

Gone – 14 – 9

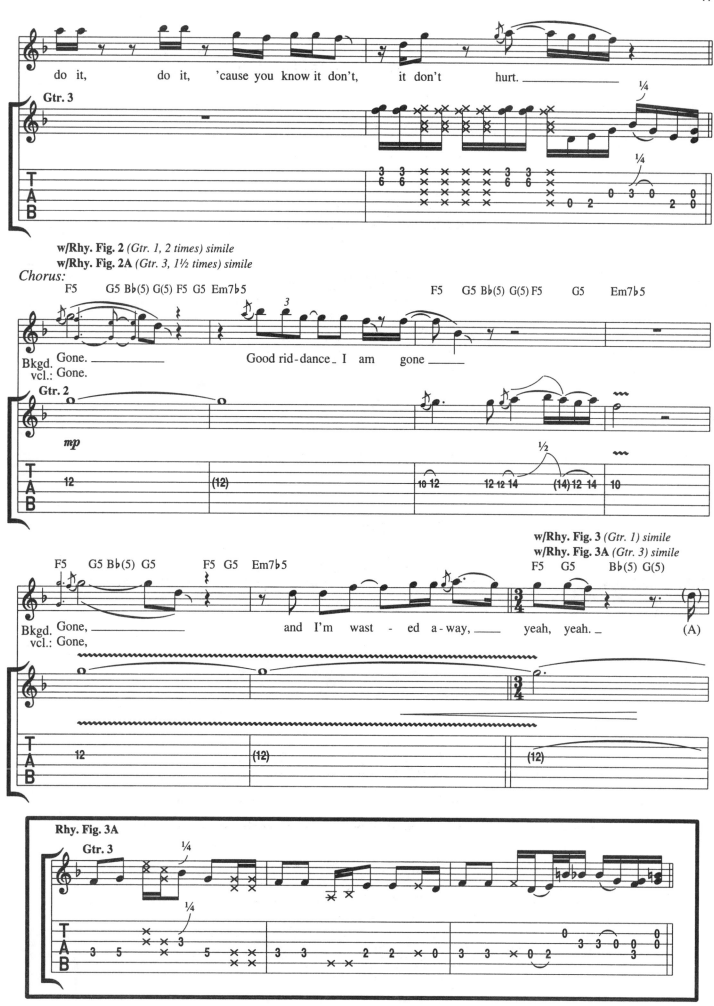

Gone – 14 – 10

48

Guitar Solo:

Gtrs 2 and 3 tacet
w/Rhy. Fig. 4 *(Gtr. 1, 8 times) simile*

wast - ed __ my way, __ I'm gone.

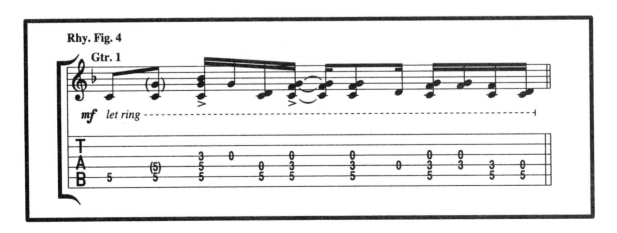

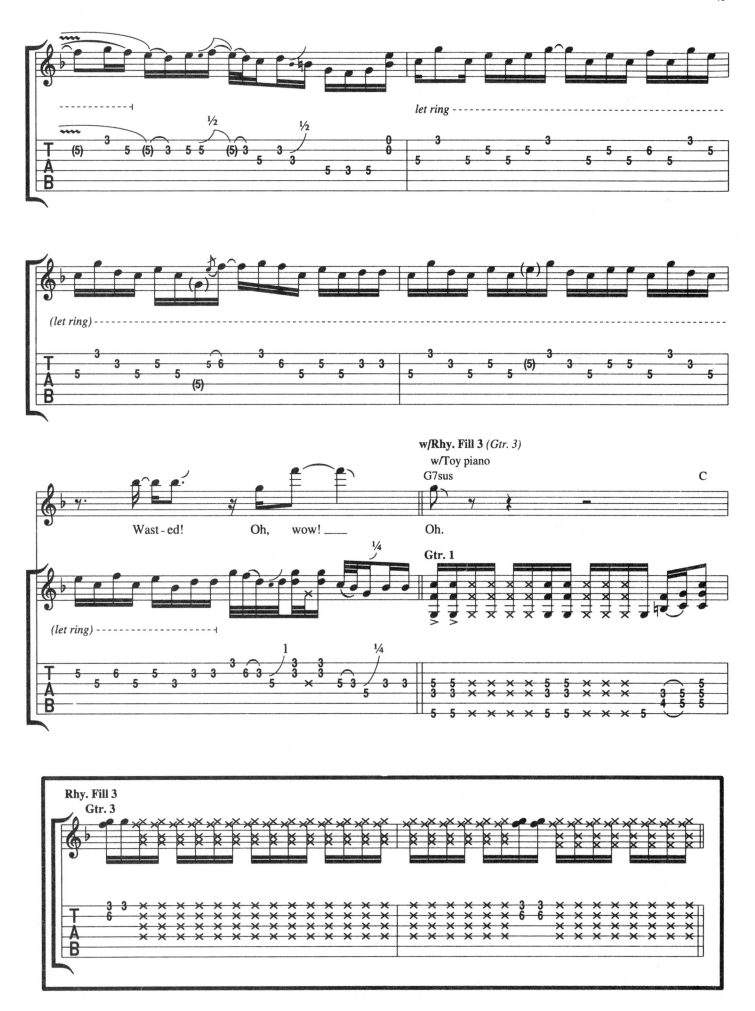

Verse 4:
Jinx me, jinx me, baby,
Beautiful like a fool.
C'mon, c'mon and remove me, baby,
Dilated and burned.

HOTEL ILLNESS

Words and Music by
CHRIS ROBINSON and
RICH ROBINSON

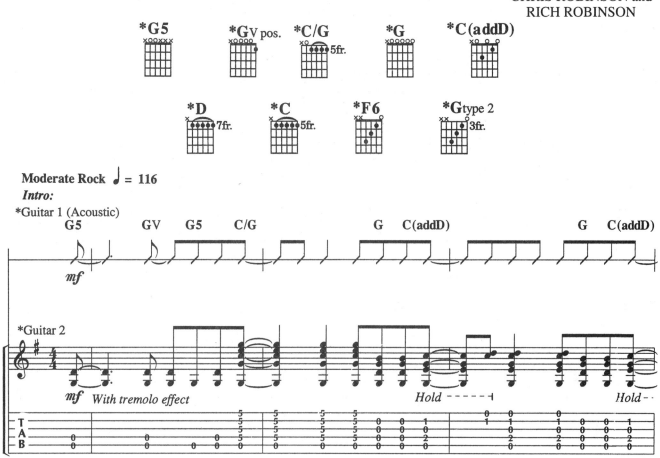

Moderate Rock ♩ = 116
Intro:
*Guitar 1 (Acoustic)

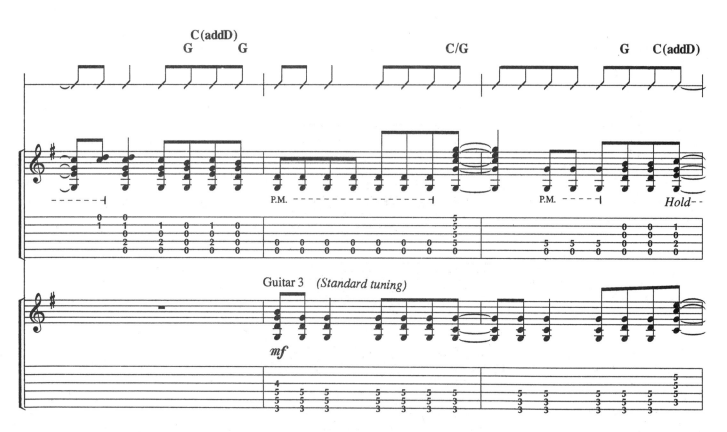

* Guitars 1 and 2 in open G tuning: ⑥ = D, ⑤ = G, ④ = D, ③ = G, ② = B, ① = D

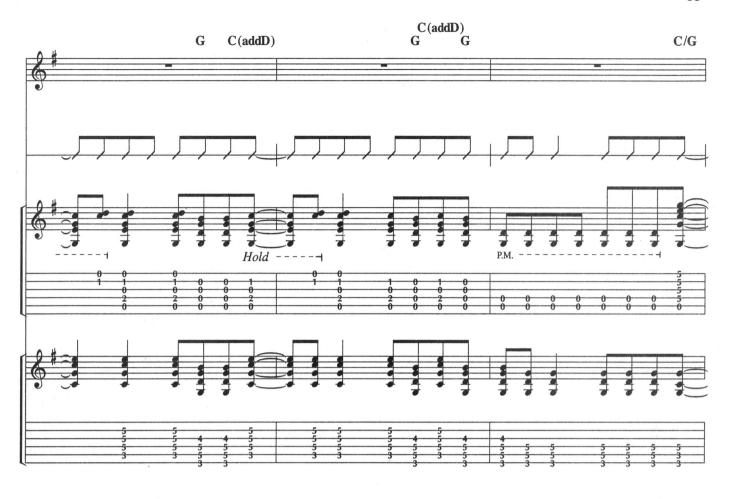

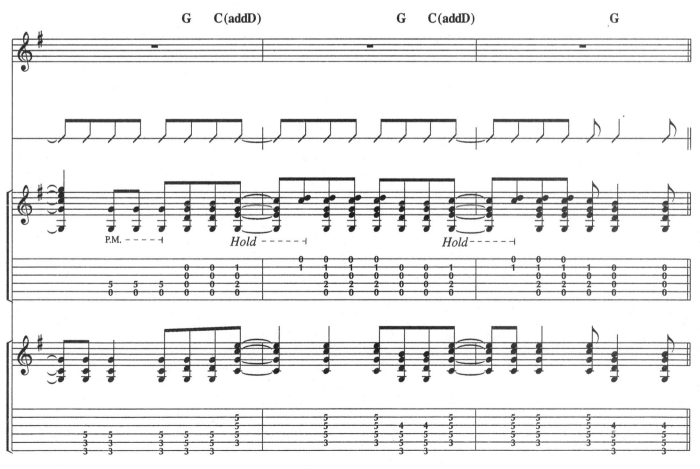

54

Verse 1:

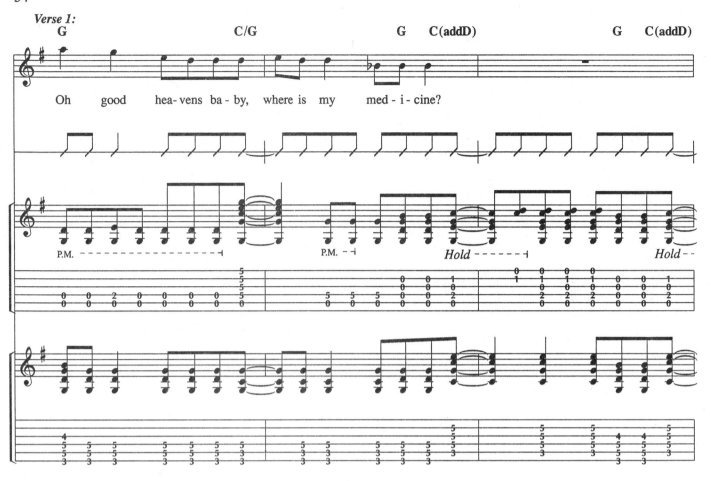

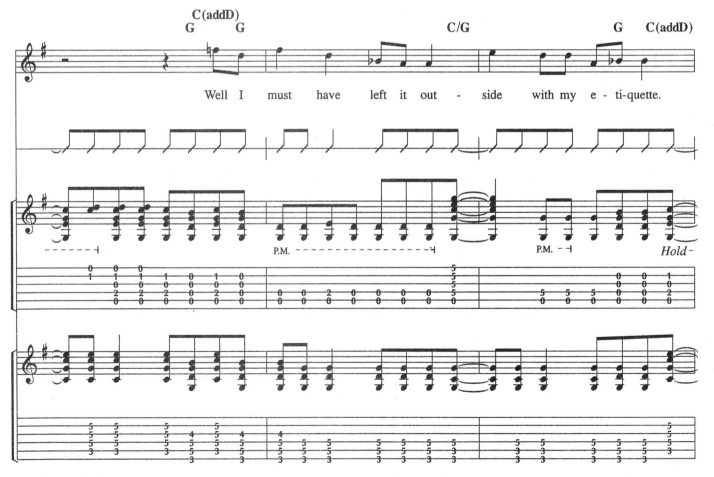

Hotel Illness - 19 - 3

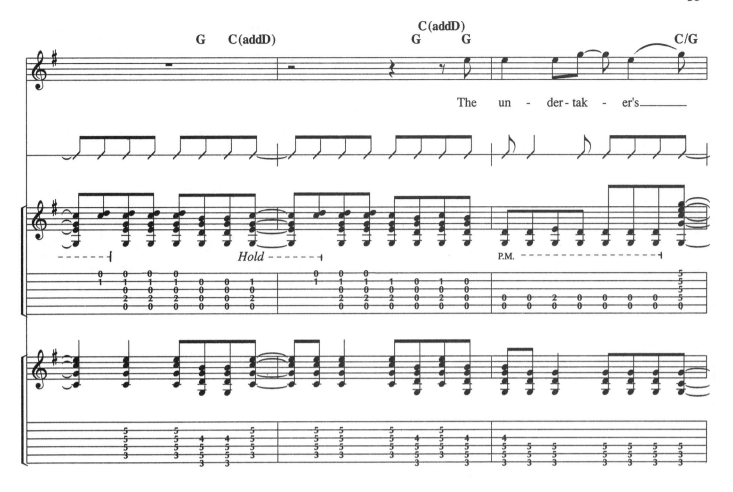

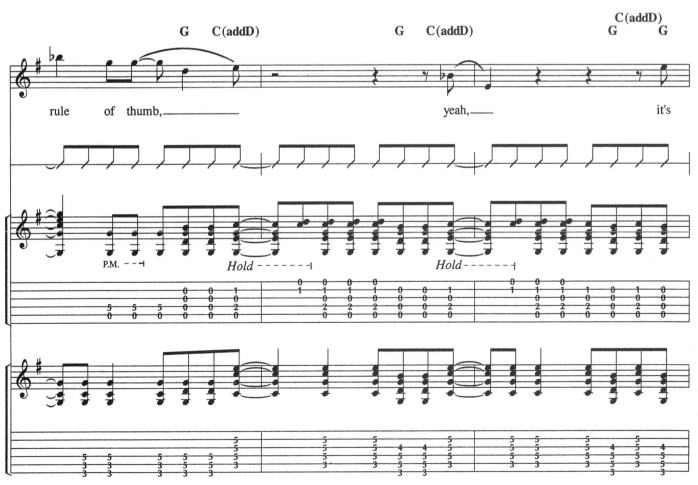

56

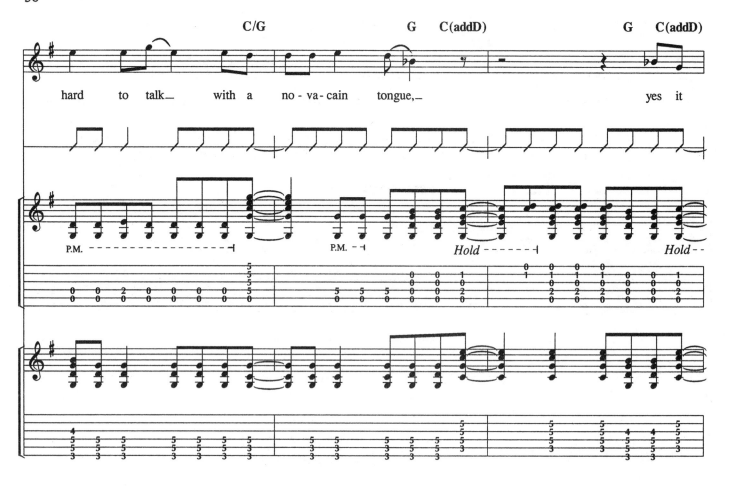

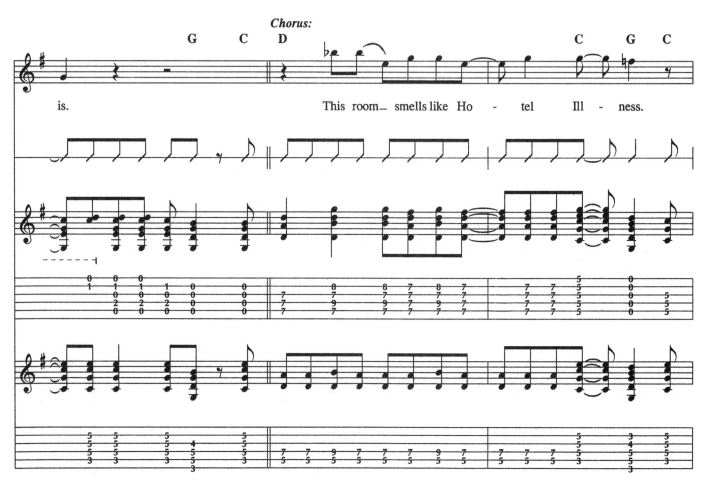

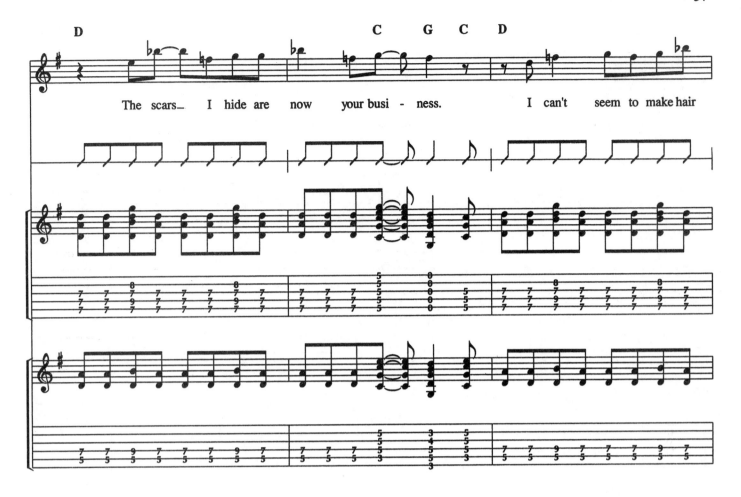

The scars__ I hide are now your busi - ness. I can't seem to make hair

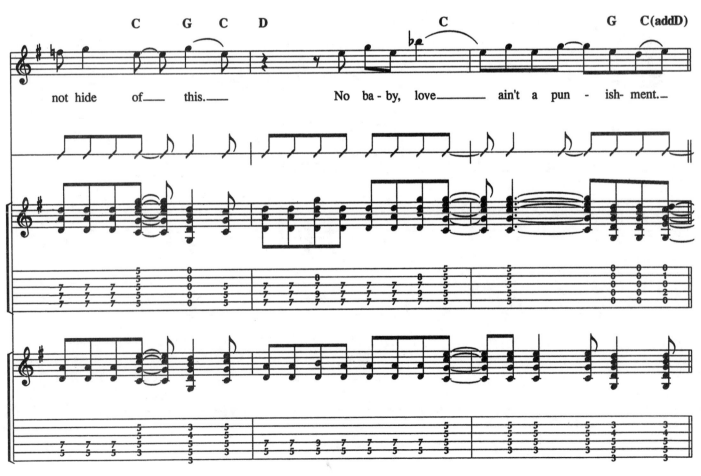

not hide of__ this.__ No ba - by, love_____ ain't a pun - ish - ment.__

58

Well,_____ this week's fash-ion is a

60

62

% *Chorus:*

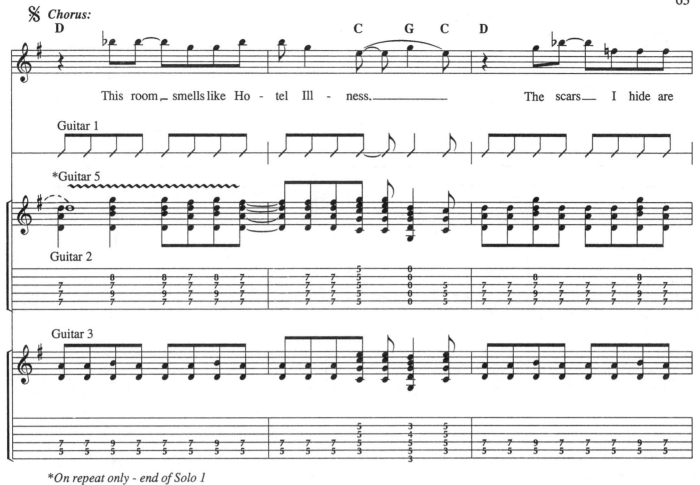

This room — smells like Ho - tel Ill - ness. — The scars — I hide are

*On repeat only - end of Solo 1

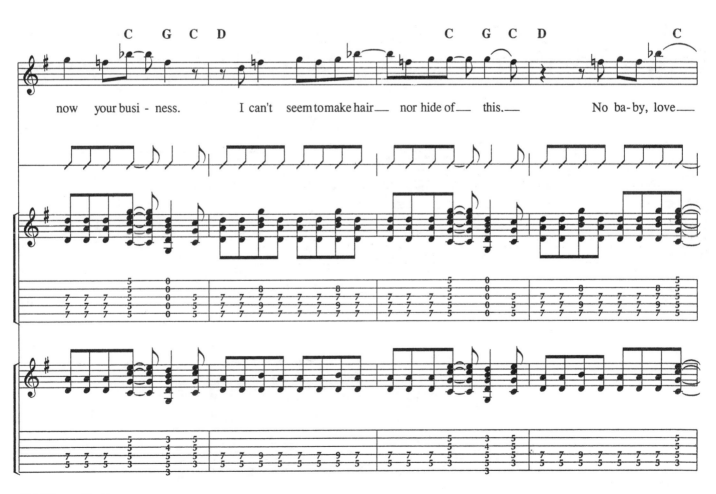

now your busi - ness. I can't seem to make hair — nor hide of — this. — No ba-by, love —

64

Hotel Illness - 19 - 13

With Fill 1(on repeat only)   *To Coda*

all those   things____   that they say   a - bout____   you?____

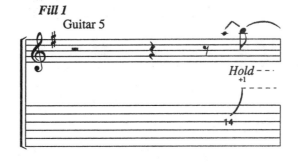

Guitar Solo 1:

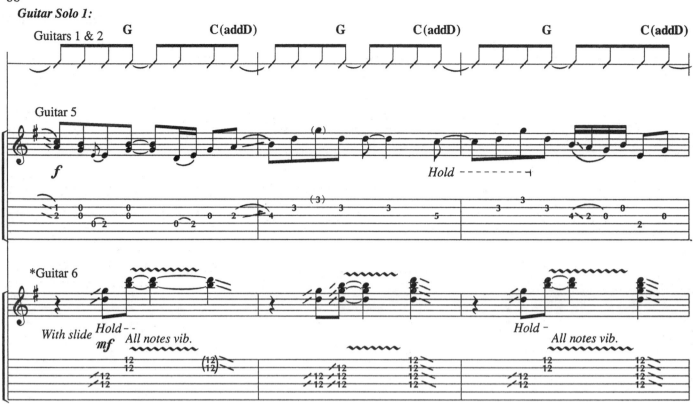

* *Guitar 6 in open G tuning:* ⑥ = D, ⑤ = G, ④ = D, ③ = G, ② = B, ① = D

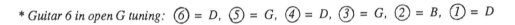

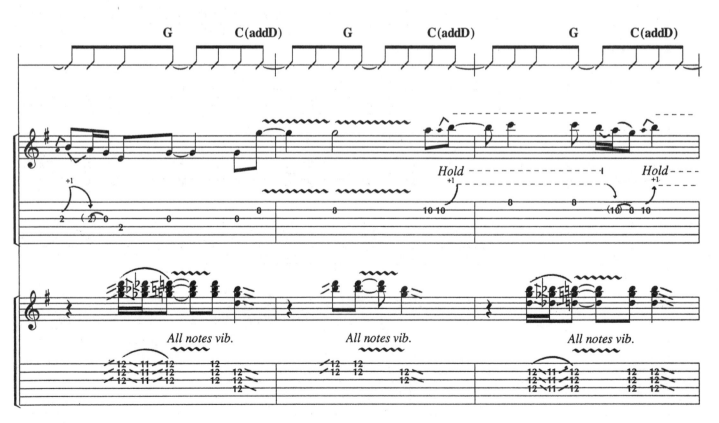

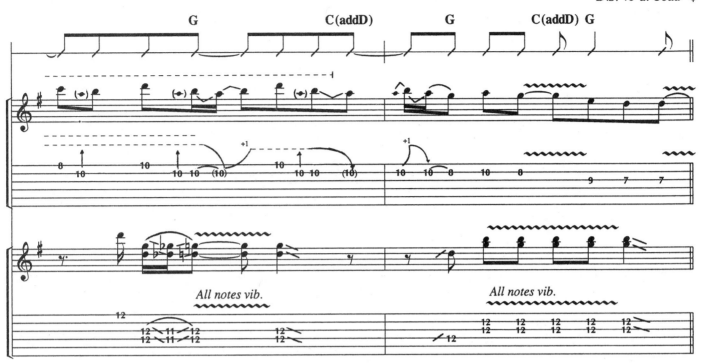

Coda

⊕ *Guitar Solo 2:*

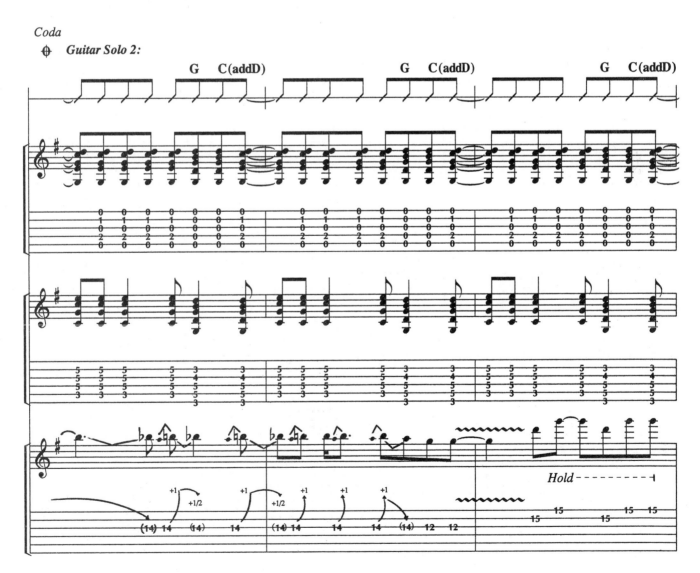

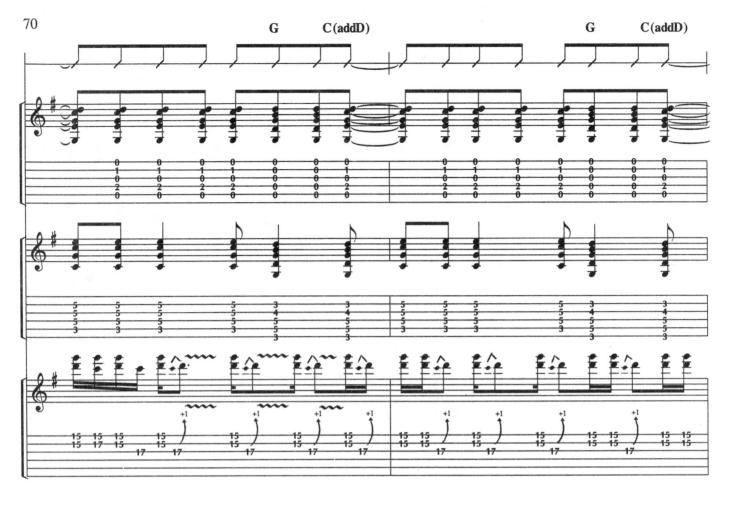

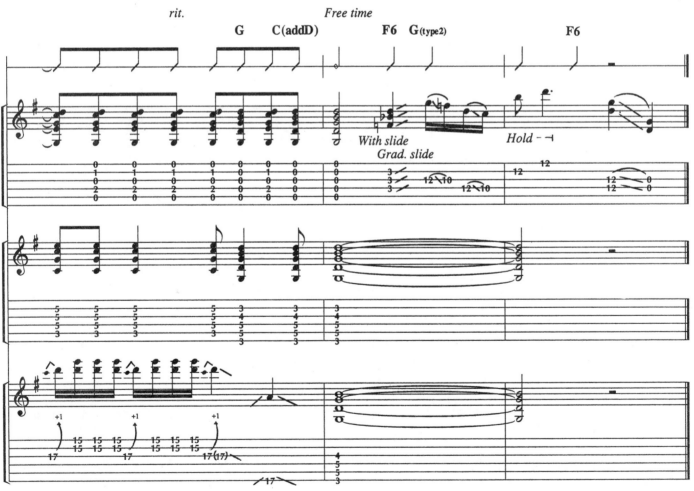

KICKING MY HEART AROUND

All gtrs. in open G tuning
tuned down 1/2 step:

⑥ = D♭   ③ = G♭
⑤ = G♭   ② = B♭
④ = D♭   ① = G♭

Words and Music by
CHRIS ROBINSON and
RICH ROBINSON

Kicking My Heart Around - 13 - 1

72

Look out!_

steady gliss.

Elec. Gtr. 3 tacet

w/**Rhy. Figs. 1** (*Elec. Gtr. 1*) & **1A** (*Elec. Gtr. 2*)
both 3 times

Elec. Gtr. 2
Rhy. Fig. 1A

Elec. Gtr. 1
Rhy. Fig. 1

w/slide

74

*Elec. Gtr. 2 simile 2nd time.

Kicking My Heart Around - 13 - 4

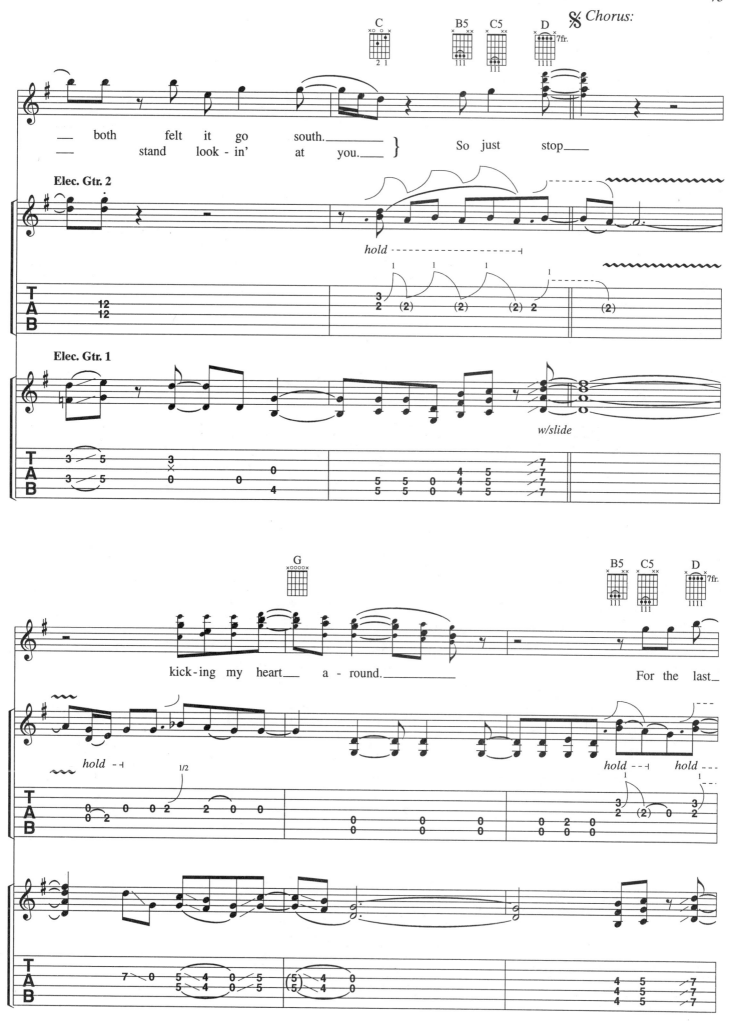

77

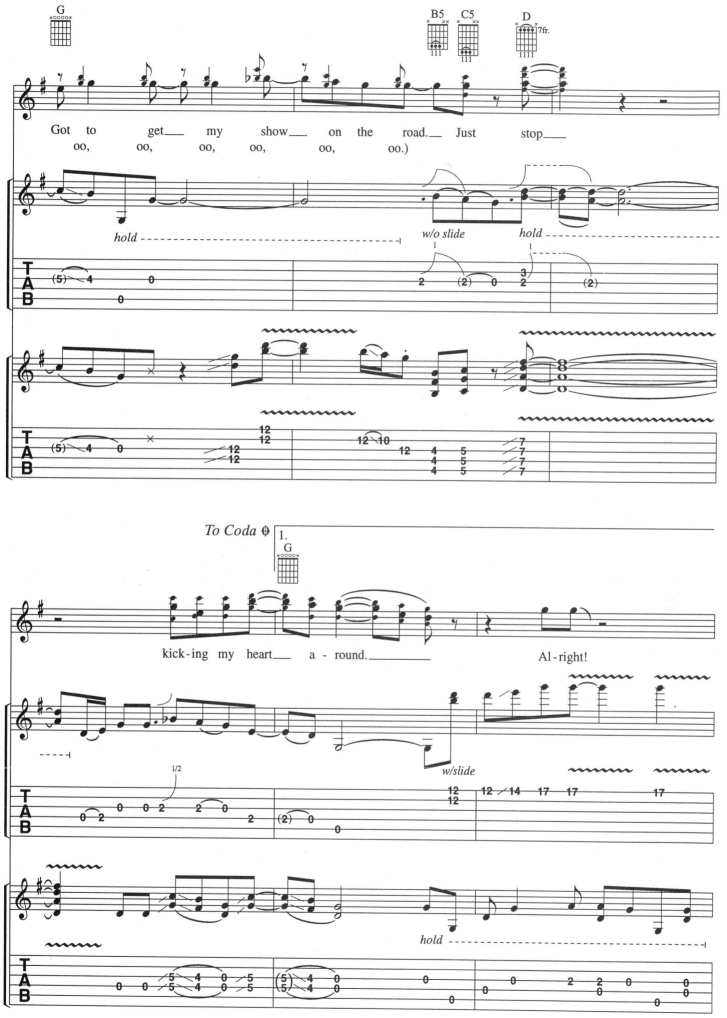

Kicking My Heart Around - 13 - 7

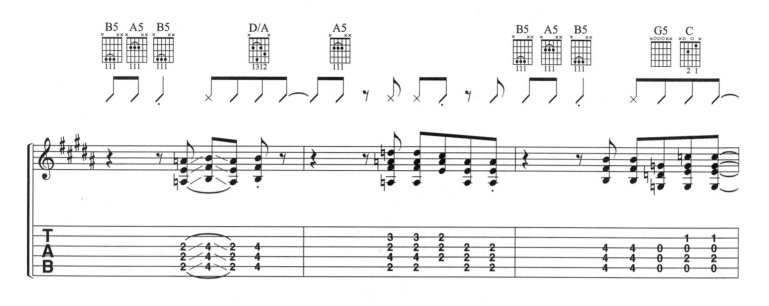

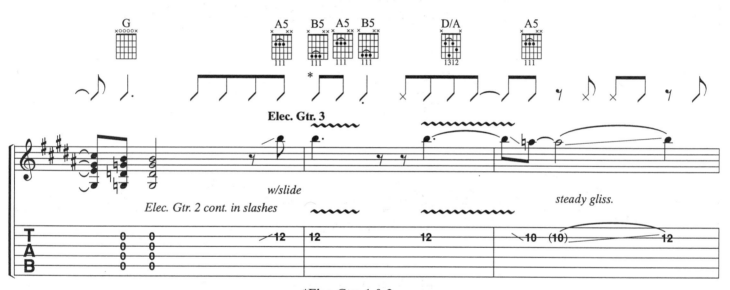

*Elec. Gtrs. 1 & 2.

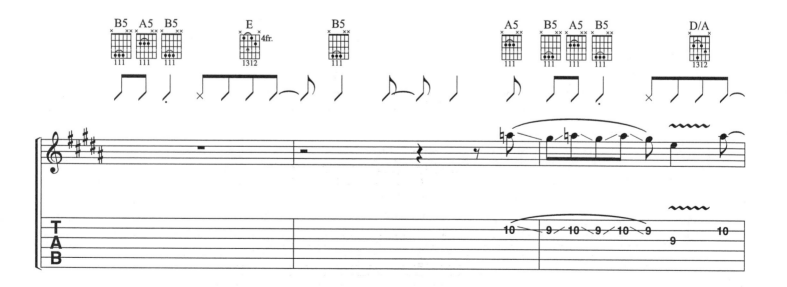

80

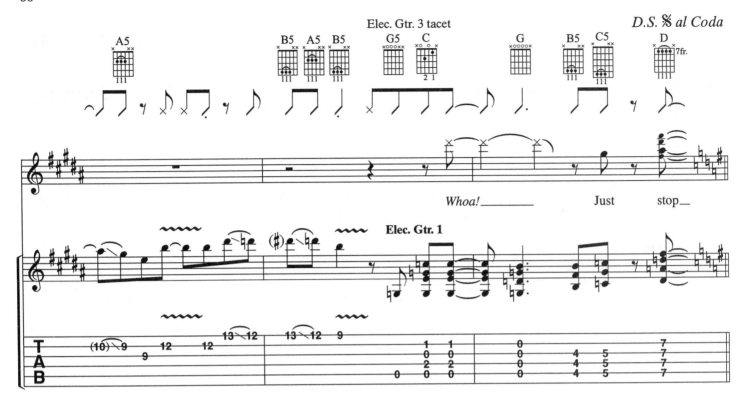

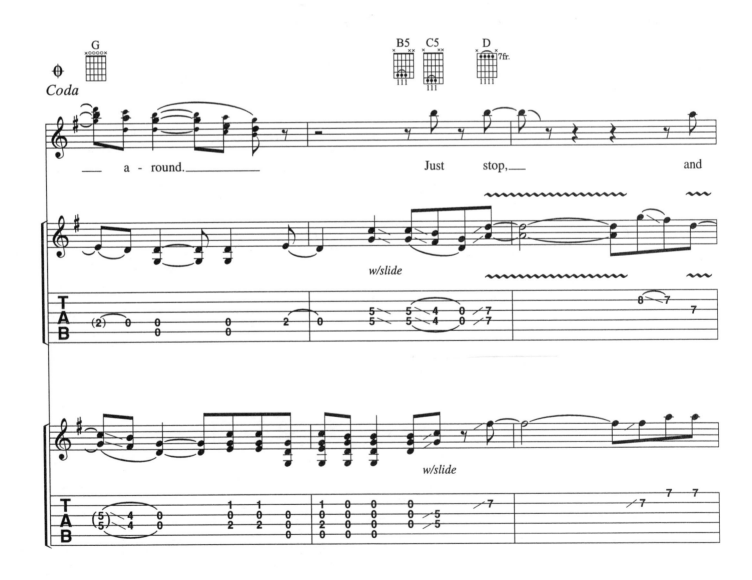

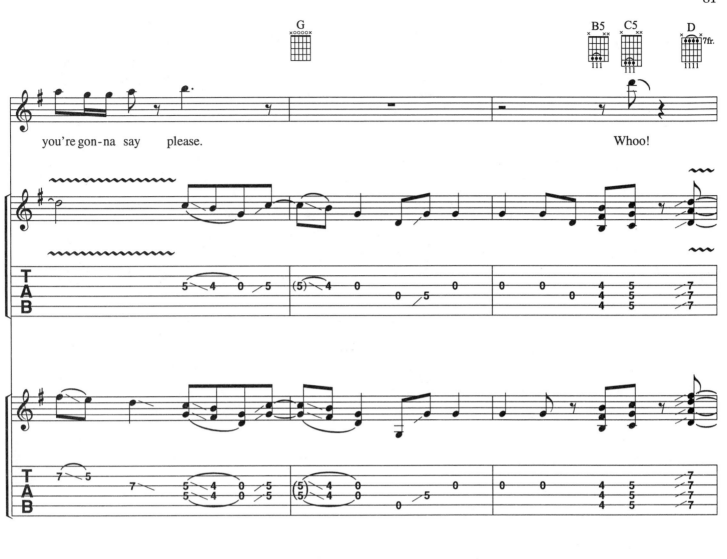

you're gon-na say   please.   Whoo!

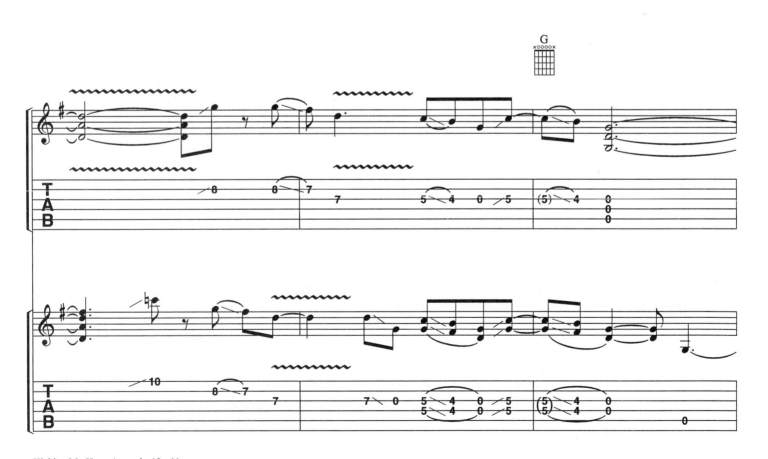

Outro:
w/Rhy. Figs. 1 *(Elec. Gtr. 1)* **& 1A** *(Elec. Gtr. 2) both 3 times*

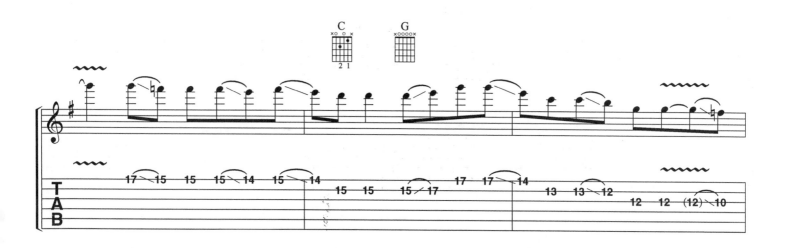

ONLY A FOOL

Words and Music by
CHRIS ROBINSON and
RICH ROBINSON

All gtrs. in open G tuning:

⑥ = D   ③ = G
⑤ = G   ② = B
④ = D   ① = D

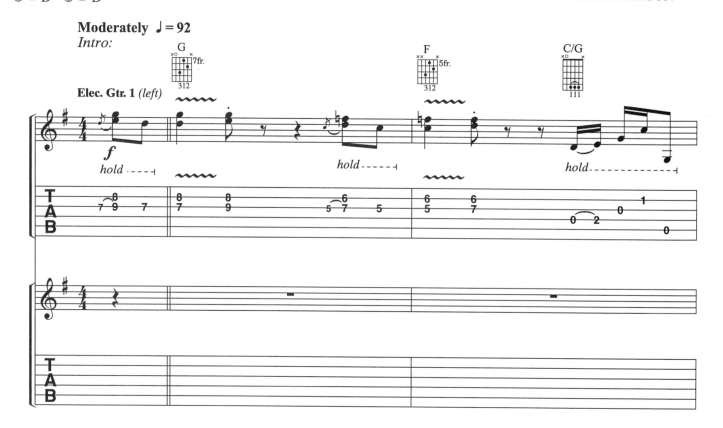

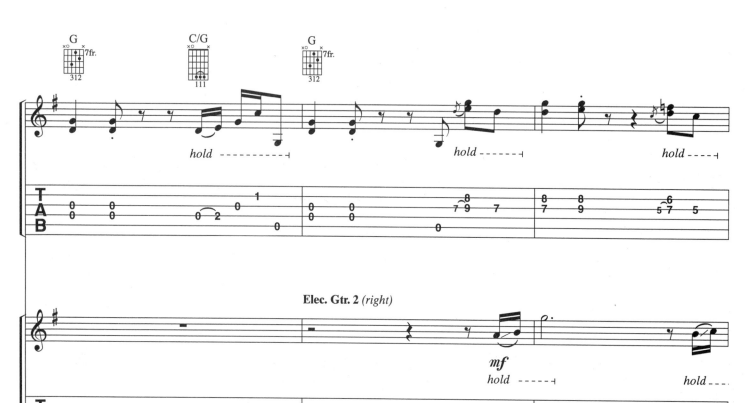

Only a Fool - 10 - 1

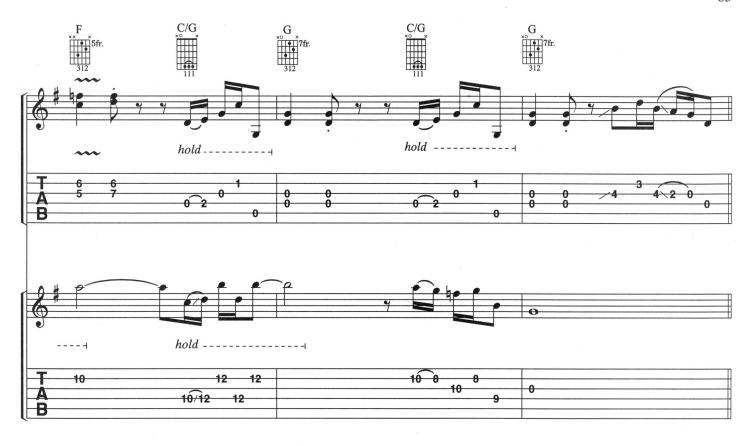

Verse:

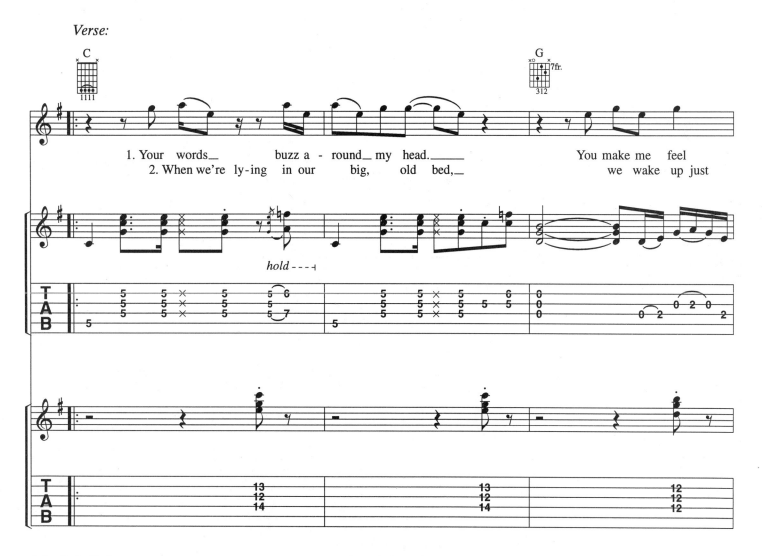

1. Your words___ buzz a - round___ my head._____ You make me feel
2. When we're ly-ing in our big, old bed,__ we wake up just

Only a Fool - 10 - 2

86

88

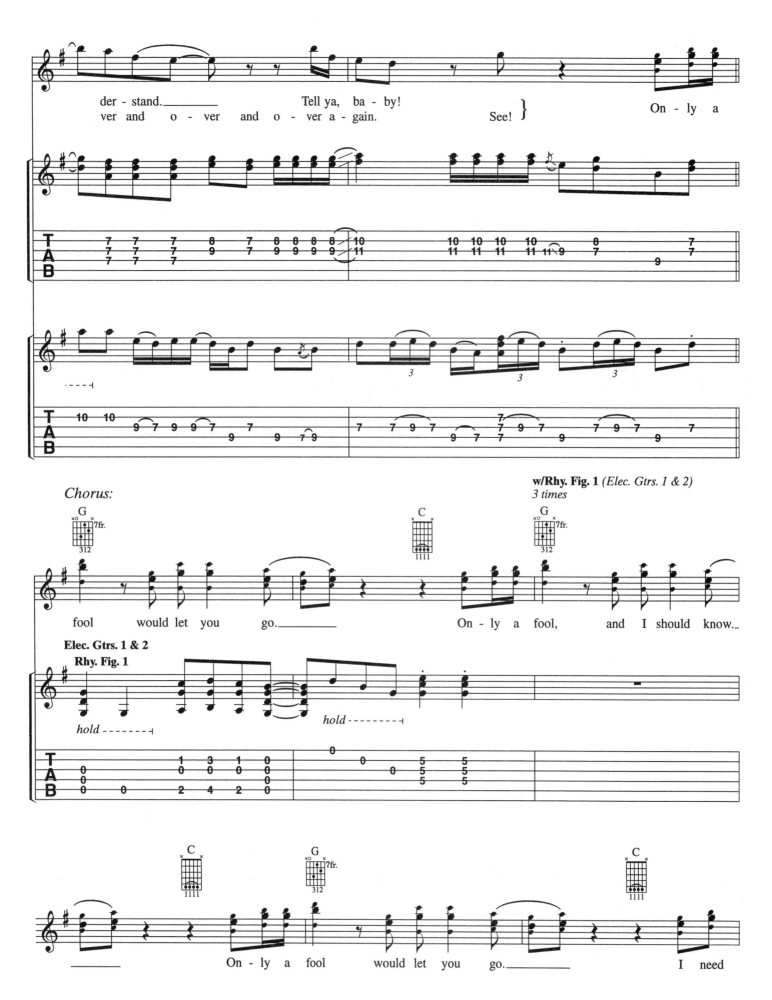

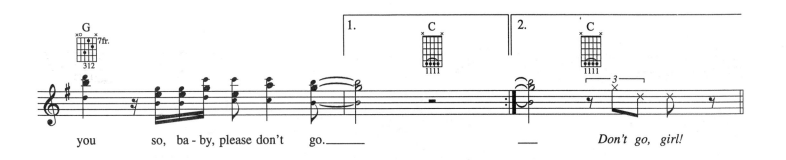

you   so, ba - by, please don't   go._____   —   *Don't go, girl!*

Guitar Solo:

90

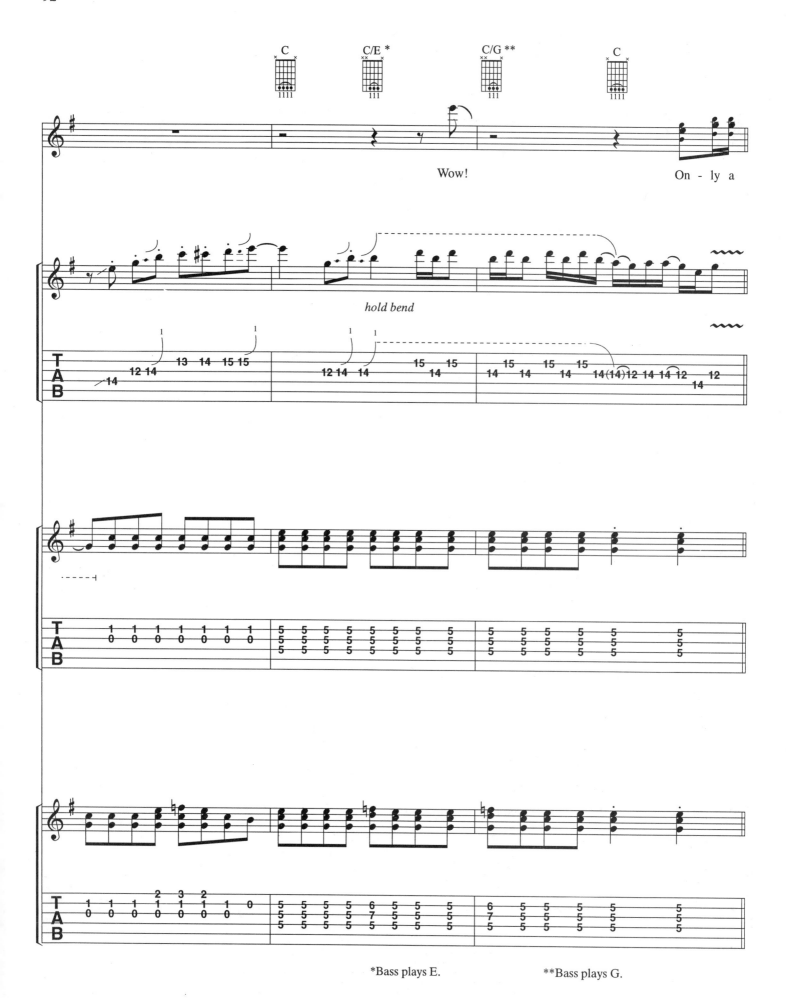

92

Wow!

On - ly a

hold bend

*Bass plays E.   **Bass plays G.

Only a Fool - 10 - 9

Chorus:
w/Rhy. Fig. 1 *(Elec. Gtrs. 1 & 2) 4 times*

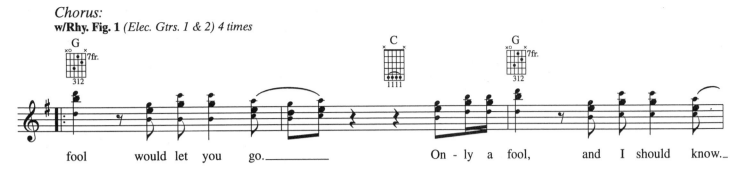

fool would let you go._____ On - ly a fool, and I should know._

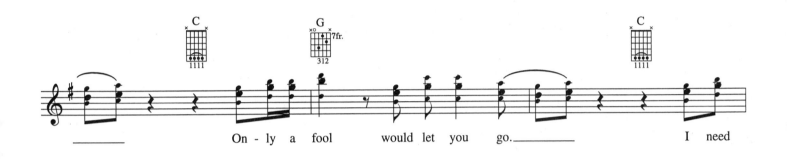

_____ On - ly a fool would let you go._____ I need

1.

you so, ba - by, please don't go._____ On - ly a

2.

you so, ba - by, please don't go.

Elec. Gtrs. 1 & 2   **Elec. Gtr. 1 only**

REMEDY

Words and Music by
CHRIS ROBINSON and
RICH ROBINSON

Moderate Rock ♩ = 80
Intro:

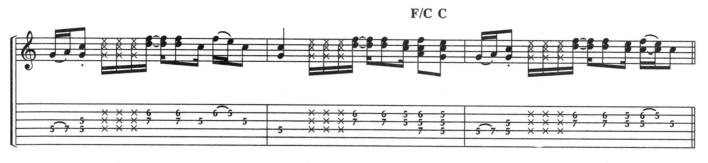

* Two Guitars arranged as one

Remedy - 9 - 1

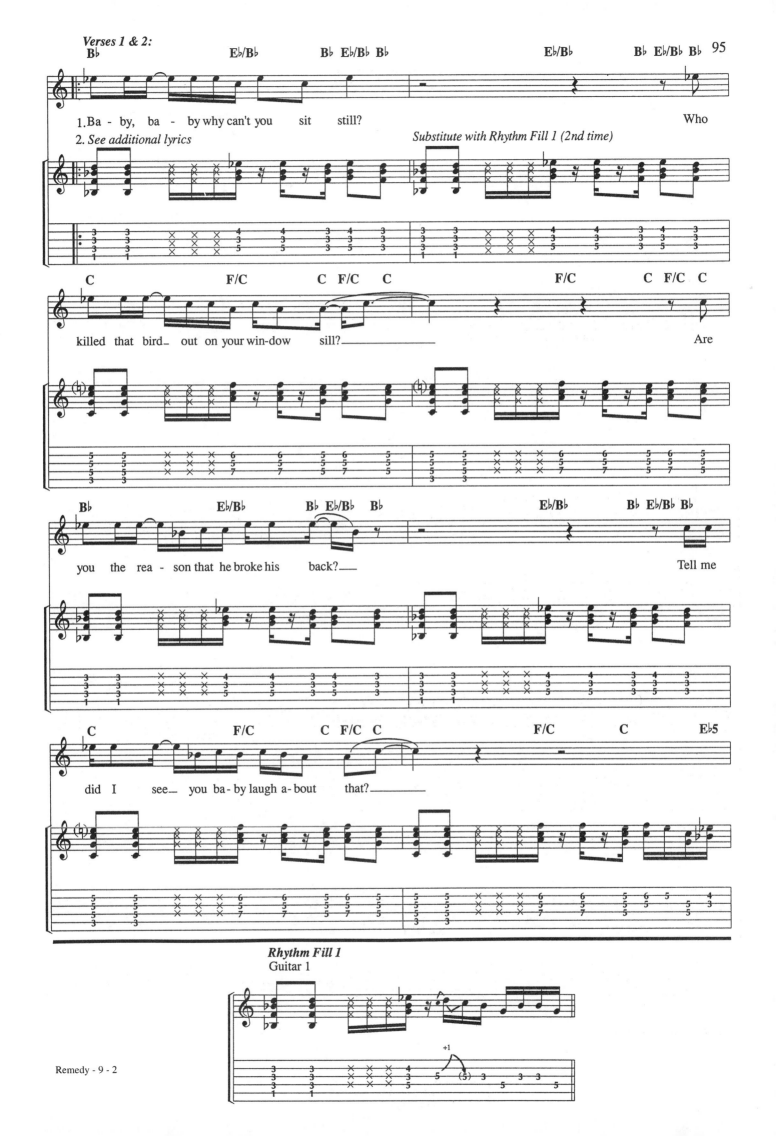

96

Substitute with Rhythm Fill 2 on repeat.

Remedy - 9 - 3

97

Remedy - 9 - 4

98

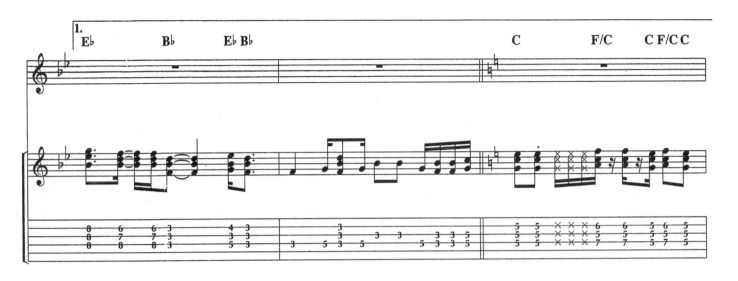

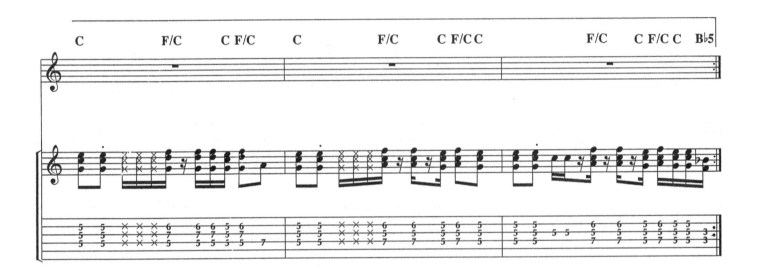

Guitar Solo

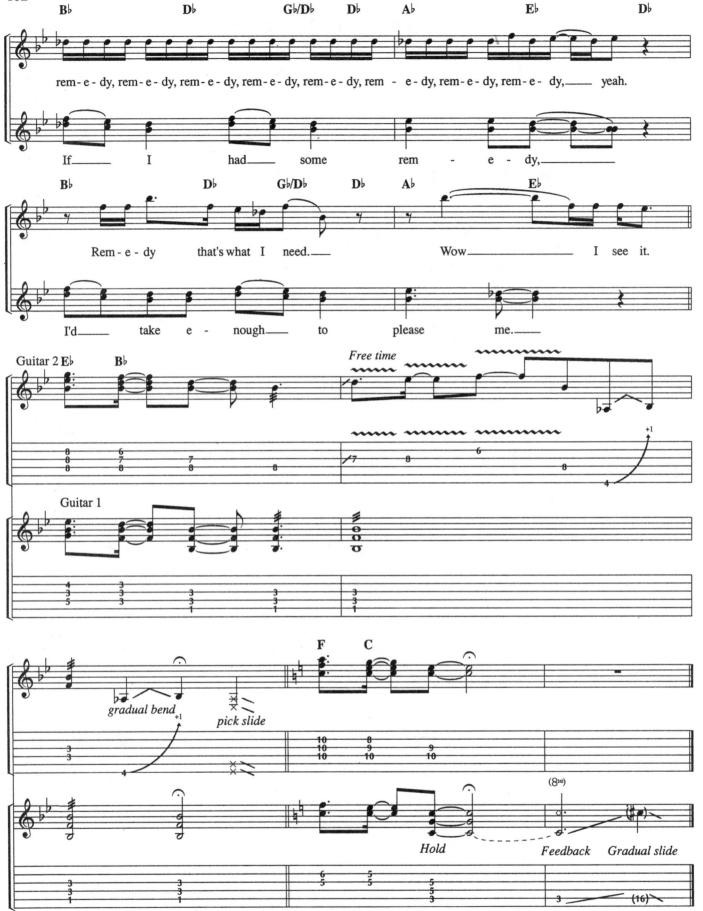

Additional Lyrics

Verse 2: Baby, baby why did you dye your hair?
Why you always keeping with your mothers dare?
Baby why's who's who, who knows you too?
Did the other children scold on you?
If I come on like a dream, would you let me show you what I mean?
If you let me come on inside,
Will you let it slide?

SEEING THINGS

Words and Music by
CHRIS ROBINSON and
RICH ROBINSON

*Use open G tuning (low to high): D G D G B D and place capo at 2nd fret.
TAB numbers shown are actual fret numbers. A "2" in TAB is thought
of as an open string.

*Standard tuning

Seeing Things - 7 - 1

104

108

Seeing Things - 7 - 6

Additional Lyrics

2. A hundred years will never ease.
   Hearin' things I won't believe.
   I saw it with my own two eyes.
   All the pain I can't hide.
   And this pain starts in my heart.
   And this love tears us apart. *(To Pre-chorus)*

SHE TALKS TO ANGELS

Words and Music by
CHRIS ROBINSON and
RICH ROBINSON

She Talks to Angels - 4 - 1

111

She Talks to Angels - 4 - 2

112

Additional Lyrics

3. She keeps a lock of hair in her pocket.
   She wears a cross around her neck.
   The hair is from a little boy,
   And the cross from someone she has not met, well, not yet. *(To Chorus)*

4. *Repeat 2nd Verse*

SISTER LUCK

Words and Music by
CHRIS ROBINSON and
RICH ROBINSON

Sister Luck - 8 - 1

116

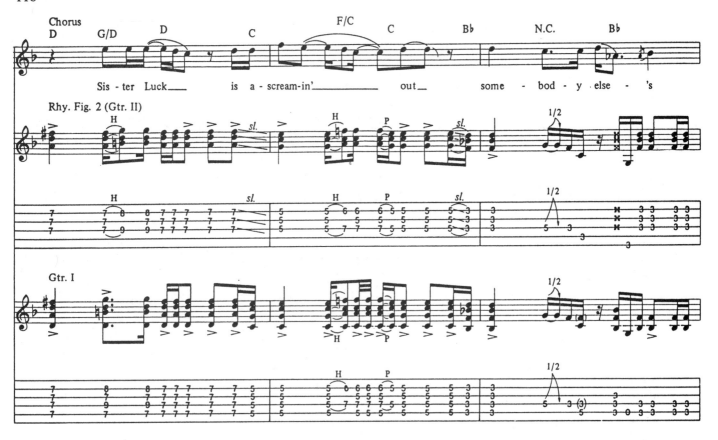

Sis - ter Luck____ is a - scream-in'_____ out____ some - bod - y else - 's

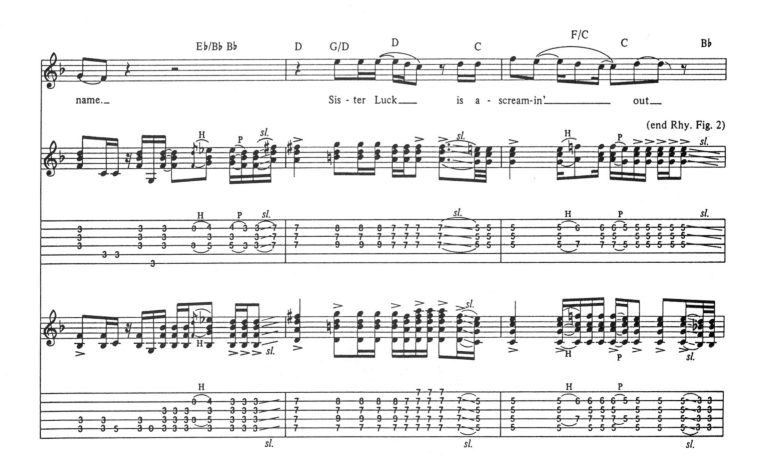

name.____ Sis - ter Luck____ is a - scream-in'_____ out____

118

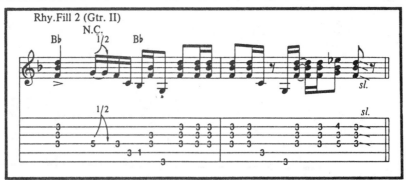

Sister Luck - 8 - 5

120

SOMETIMES SALVATION

Words and Music by
CHRIS ROBINSON and
RICH ROBINSON

Moderate Rock ♩ = 100

Verse 1:

To les - sen my trou - bles stopped hang - in' out with vul tures and emp - ty sav - iors like

Sometimes Salvation - 9 - 1

123

Sometimes Salvation - 9 - 2

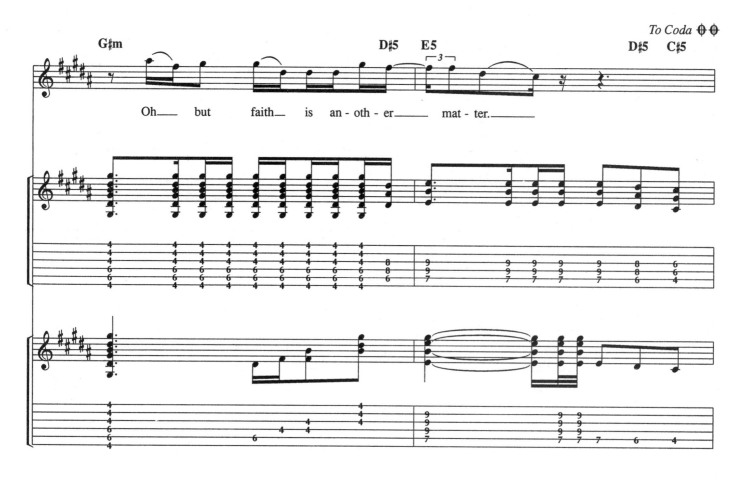

Oh___ but faith___ is an-oth-er___ mat-ter.___

Oh, so don't___ you sur - ren-der, oh, no, no.___ 'Cause

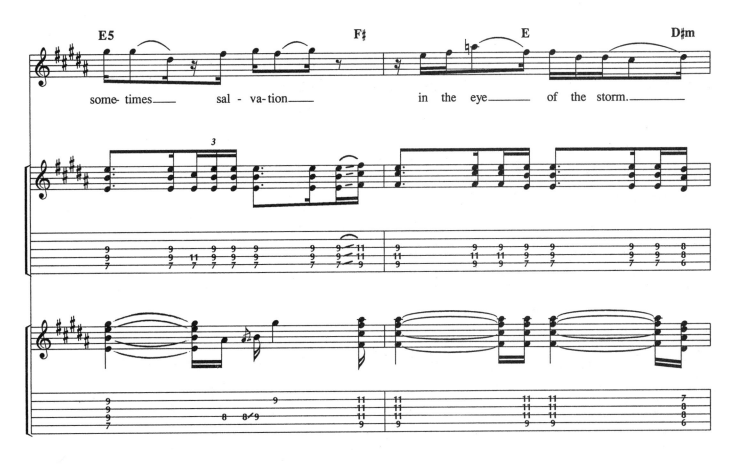

Verse 2:

I've no time for ac-cus - a-tions_ or con - ver-sa - tions on all the bad, bad_ things that you do._ Just a note_ from_ your jail - or;_ drugs in the re- la - tion_ to all_ the_ peo-ple a - round_ you._

D.S. 𝄋 al Coda

Guitar 1

Guitar 2

Hold - - - - - - - - - - - -

130

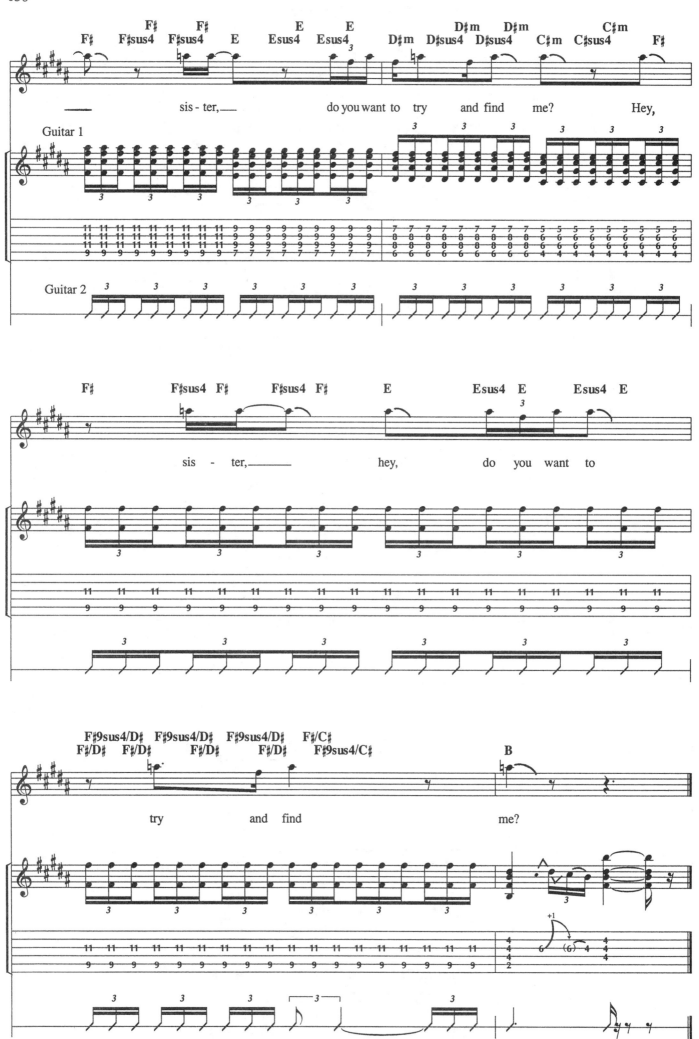

STING ME

Words and Music by
CHRIS ROBINSON and
RICH ROBINSON

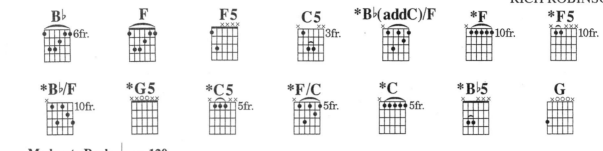

Moderate Rock ♩ = 120

Intro:

Guitar 1 Tuning: ⑥= D ⑤= G ④= D ③= G ②= B ①= D

Sting Me - 23 - 1

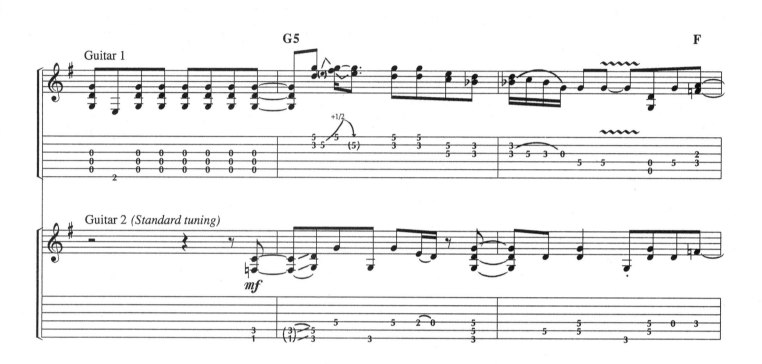

Sting Me - 23 - 2

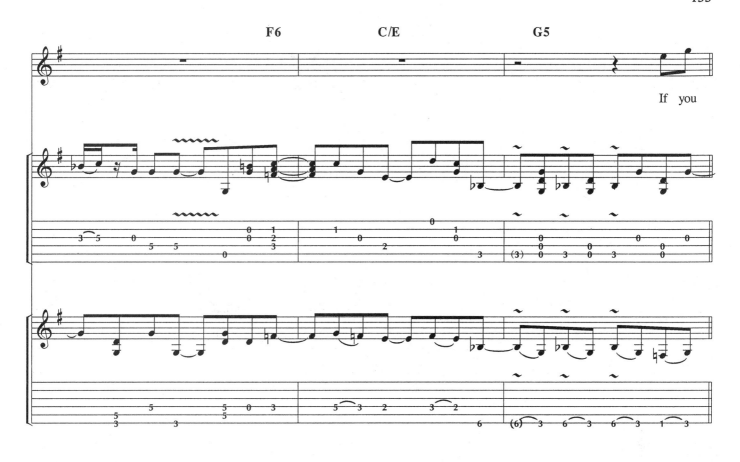

Verse 1:

feel— like a ri - ot, then don't you de — ny it.__ *Background vocal:* Put your good— foot for -

134

G5
F

No need____ for her - o - ics, I just-a want you to show__ me.____

ward.

C/E
G5

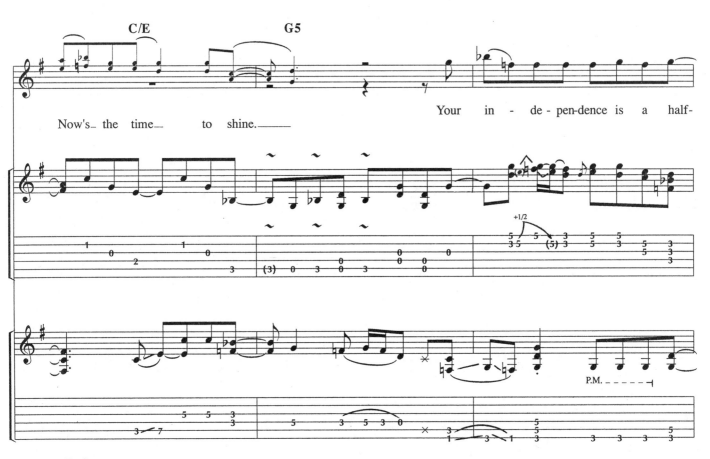

Now's_ the time__ to shine._____

Your in - de - pen-dence is a half-

Sting Me - 23 - 4

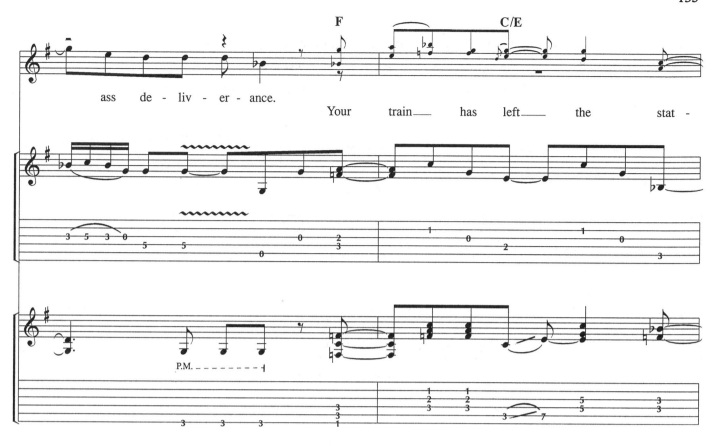

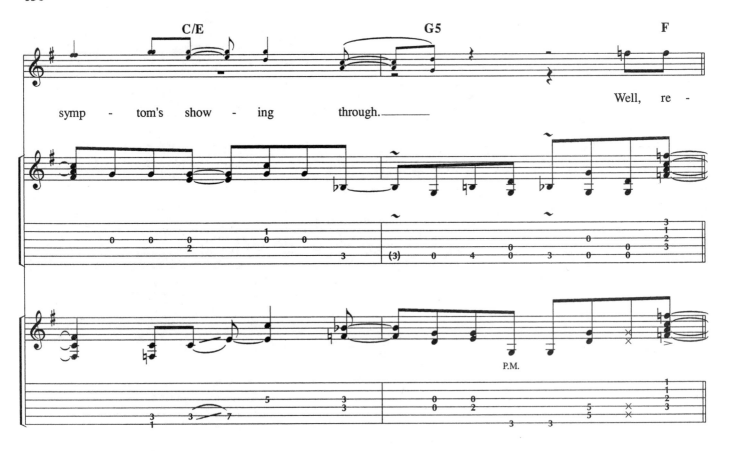

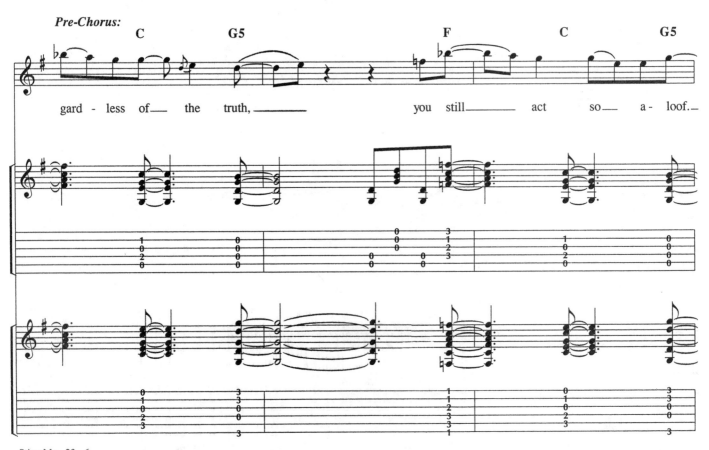

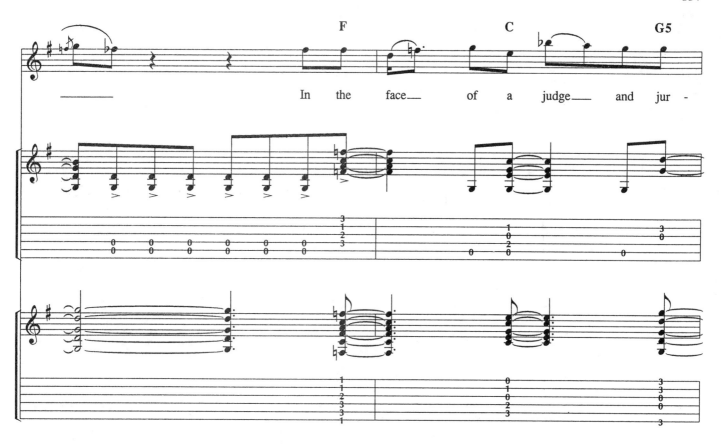

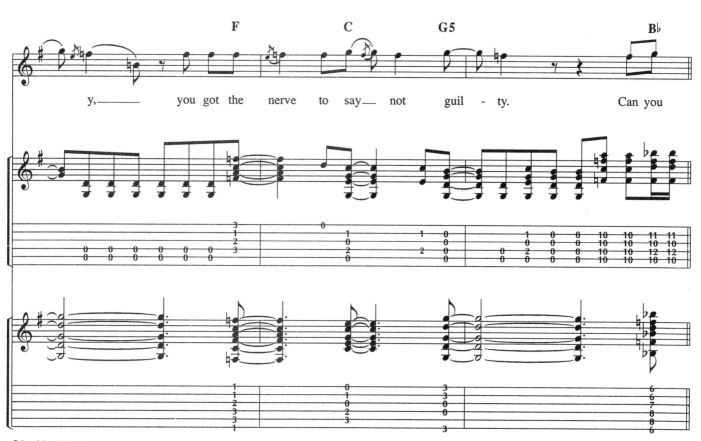

138

Chorus:

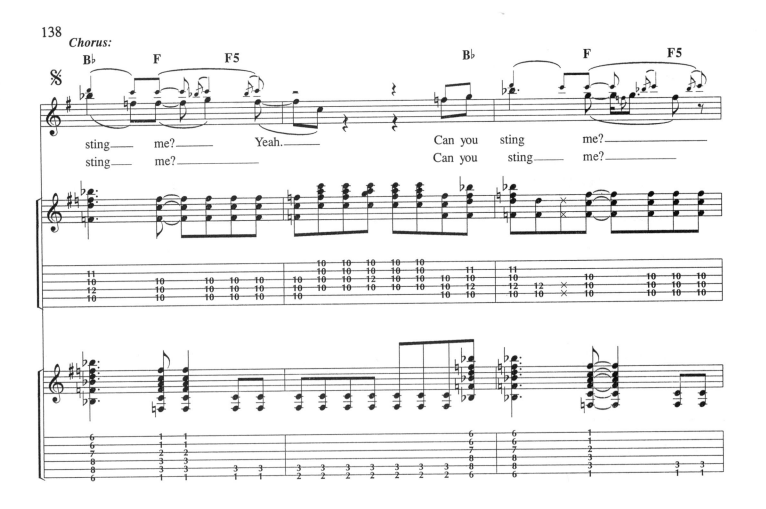

sting___ me?___ Yeah.___ Can you sting me?___
sting___ me?___ Can you sting___ me?___

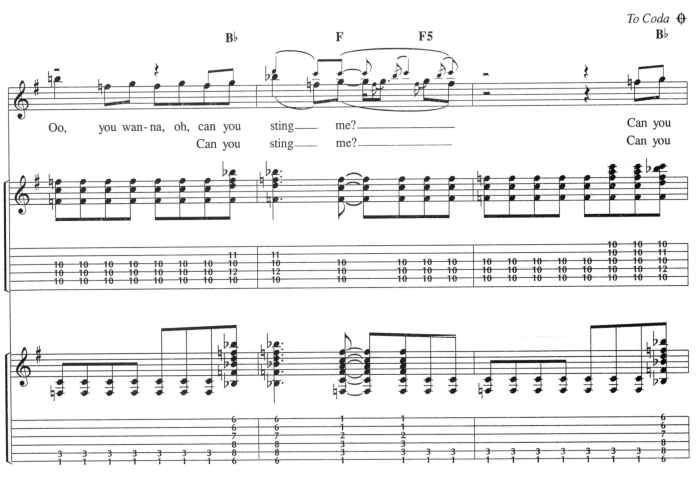

Oo, you wan-na, oh, can you sting___ me?___ Can you
Can you sting___ me?___ Can you

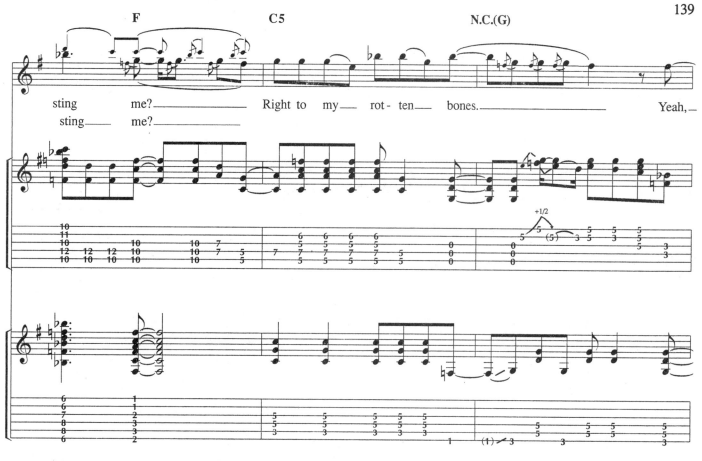

Sting Me - 23 - 9

140

(F)   (C/E)

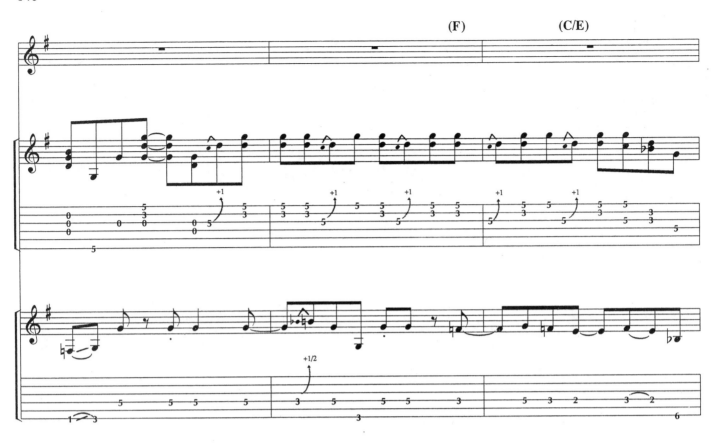

(G5)   Verse 2:
N.C.(G)   F

Well, the bell rings out for the crime of the cen-tur-y.

With improvisation

With improvisation

Sting Me - 23 - 10

F   C/E

Sons   and daugh-ters bet-ter o - pen your   eyes.___   Tell   me what_ you're   see-

G5   F(addG)

ing.   'Cause this__ sub - mis-sion is a   tired __ trad - i - tion.   It's

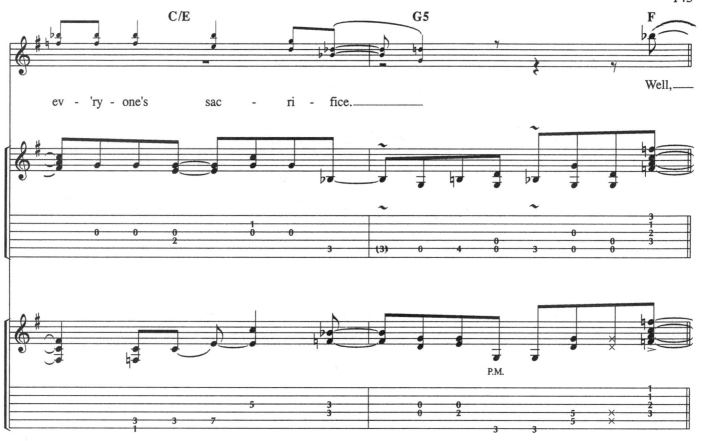

ev - 'ry - one's   sac - ri - fice._____

Well,___

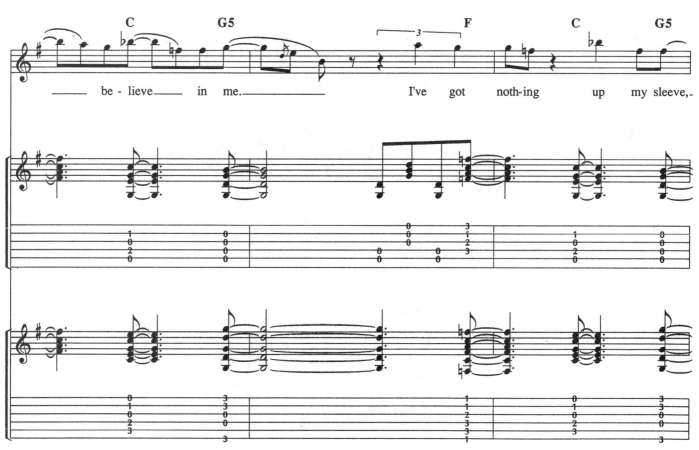

_____ be - lieve____ in me._____   I've got noth-ing   up my sleeve,-

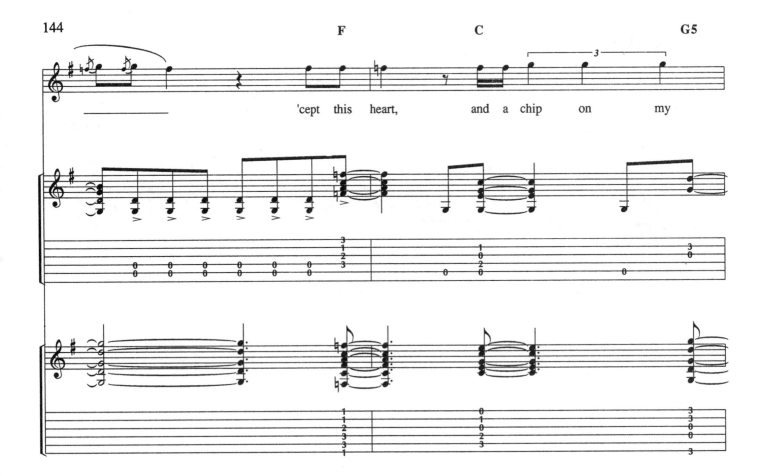

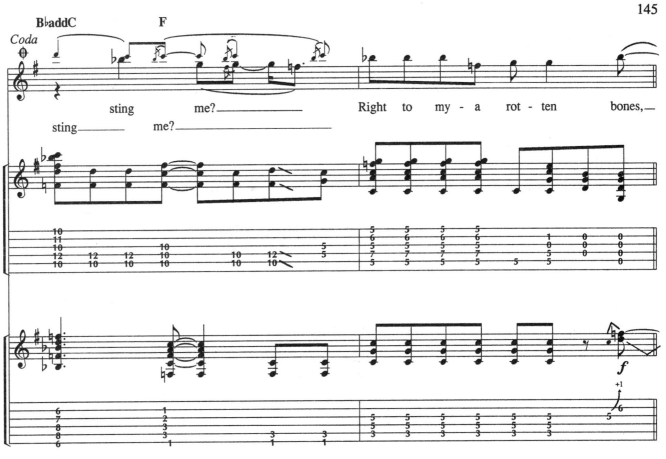

sting me?_____ Right to my - a rot-ten bones,—

sting_____ me?_____

Guitar Solo

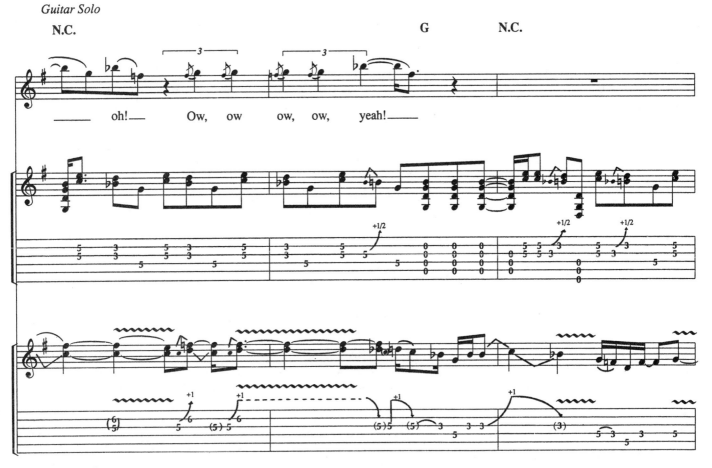

_____ oh!___ Ow, ow ow, ow, yeah!_____

146

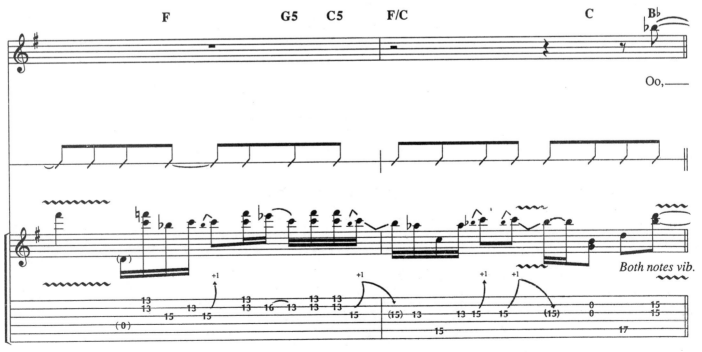

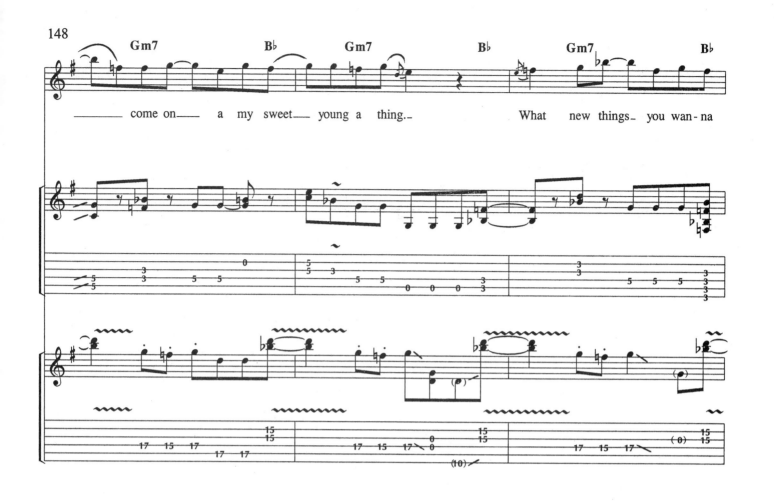

come on____ a my sweet____ young a thing.____ What new things_ you wan-na

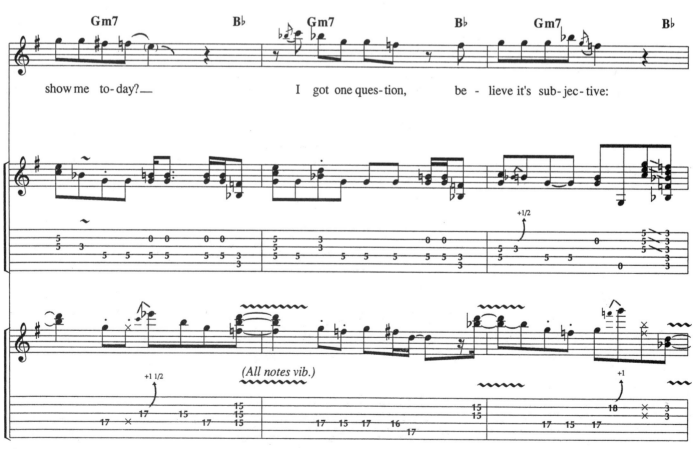

show me to-day?____ I got one ques-tion, be - lieve it's sub-jec-tive:

(All notes vib.)

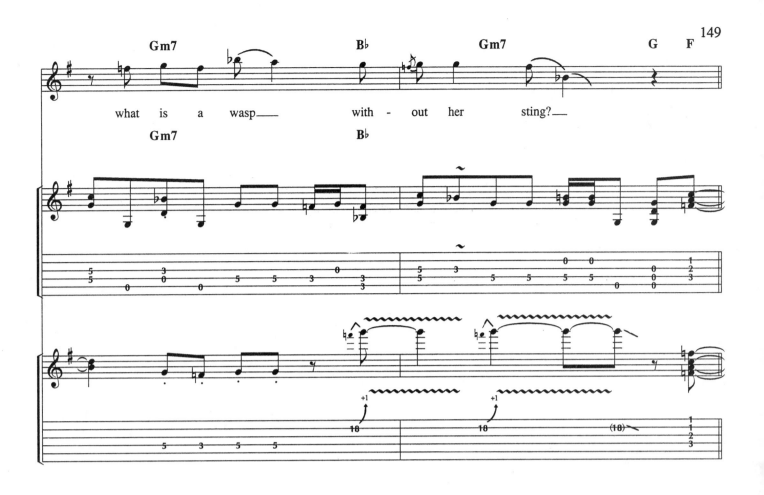

what is a wasp___ with - out her sting?___

Pre-Chorus:

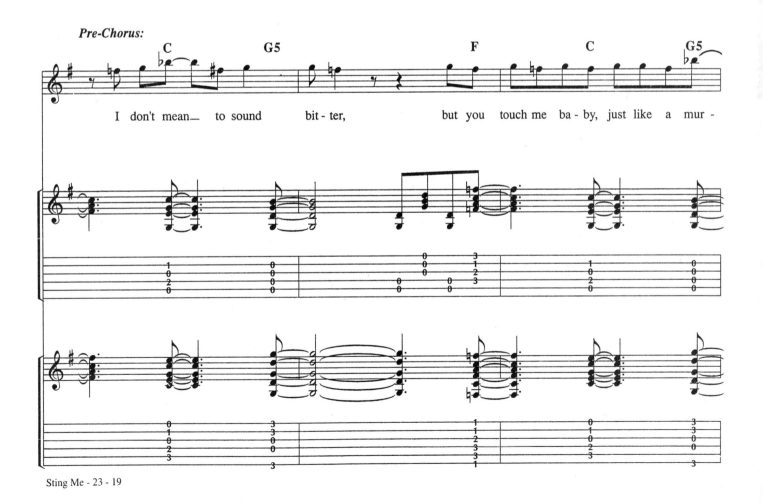

I don't mean___ to sound bit - ter, but you touch me ba - by, just like a mur -

Sting Me - 23 - 19

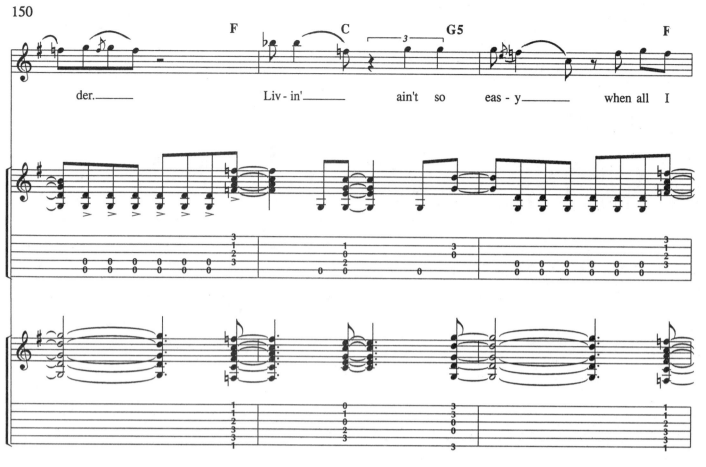

der._____ Liv-in'_____ ain't so eas-y_____ when all I

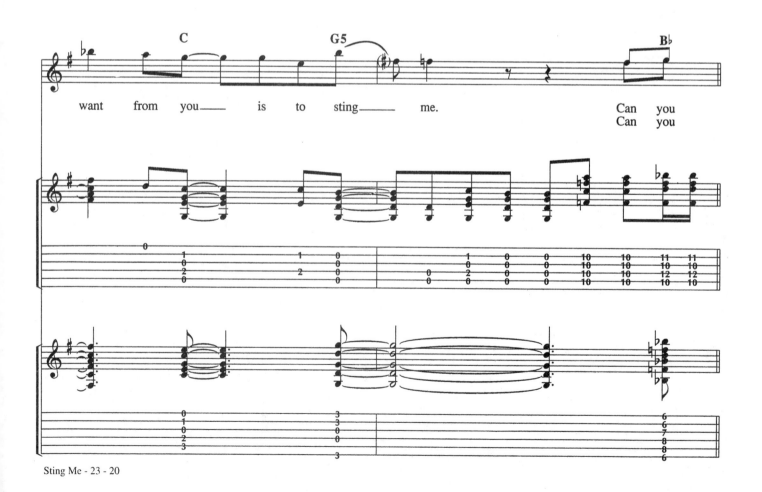

want from you____ is to sting____ me. Can you
Can you

Sting Me - 23 - 20

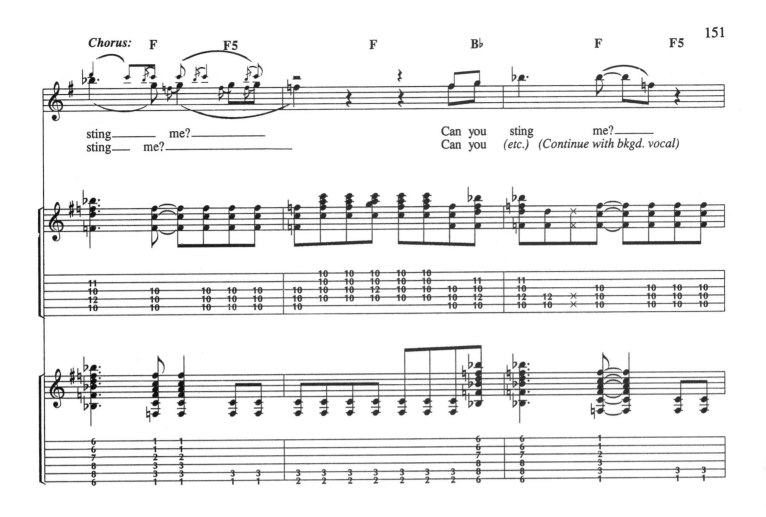

152

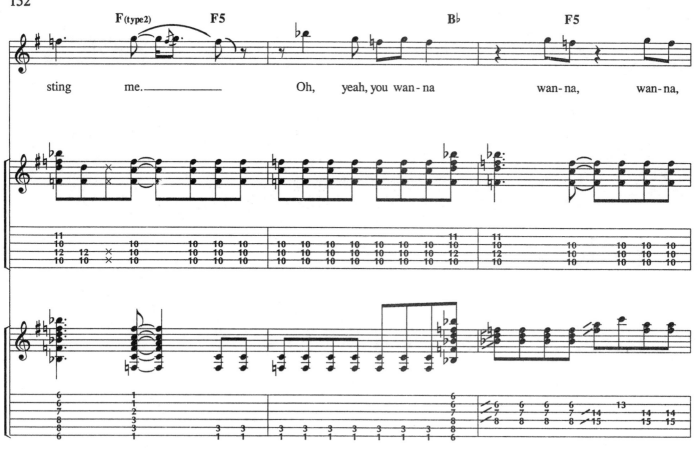

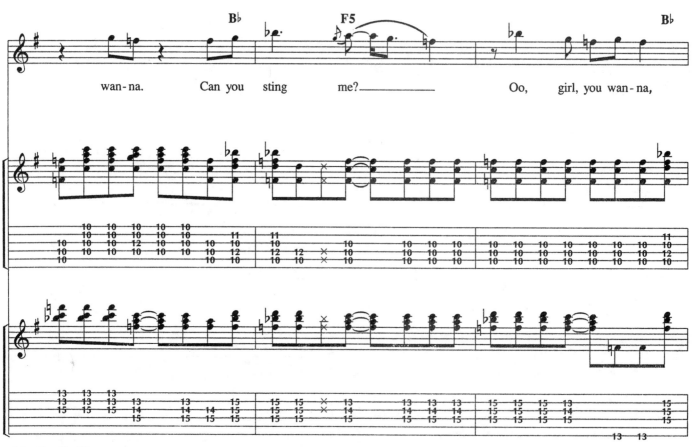

Sting Me - 23 - 22

WISER TIME

Gtrs. 2, 3 and 4 in G tuning:

⑥ = D   ③ = G
⑤ = G   ② = B
④ = D   ① = D

Words and Music by
CHRIS ROBINSON and
RICH ROBINSON

Moderately slow ♩ = 78

Gtr. 1 (semi-clean tone)
w/pedal-steel background swells

Intro:

Segue from
"Ballad in Urgency"
Drums

Rhy. Fig. 1
B♭   Am7   G

mf w/pick and fingers
let ring throughout

Rhy. Fig. 1A
Gtr. 2 (semi-clean tone)

mf let ring throughout

B♭   Am7   G

Wiser Time – 12 – 1

oth - er song ____ an - oth - er mile. _____ Oh, yeah. ____

158

Wiser Time – 12 – 5

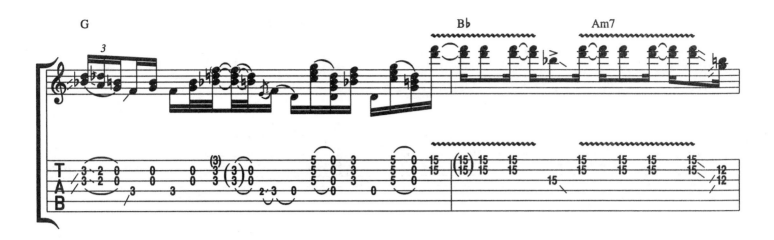

Keyboard Solo:

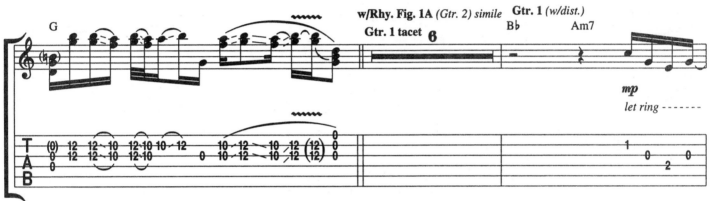

Guitar Solo:

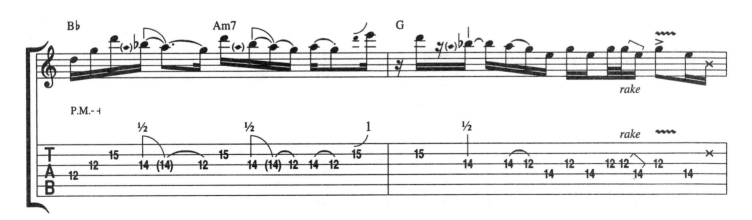

162

Wiser Time – 12 – 9

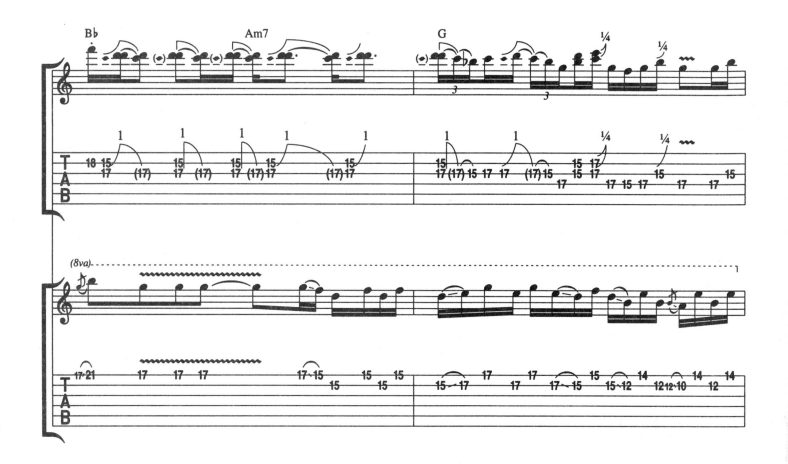

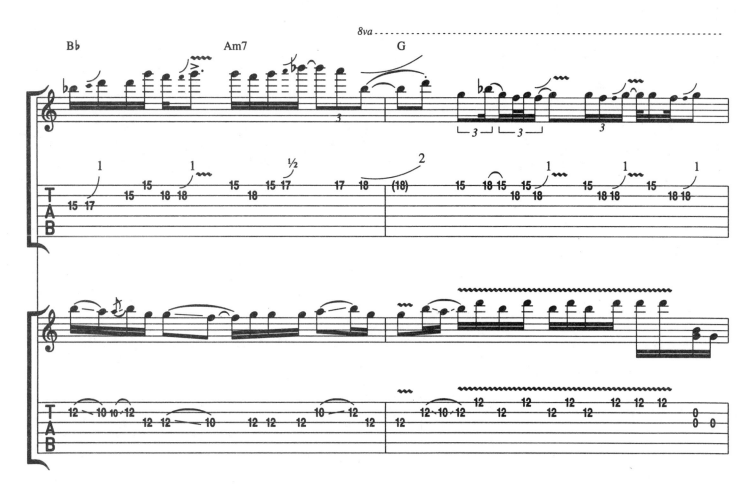

Outro Chorus:

w/Rhy. Fig. 2 *(Gtr. 1, 2 times) simile*
w/Rhy. Fig. 2A *(Gtr. 2, 3¾ times) simile*

Gtr. 4 ad lib. to end

And on a good day, _____ well, I know it ain't ev-'ry day _ we _

_ can _ part _ the sea. _____ And e-ven on a bad day _

well, I know it ain't ev-'ry day _____ glo - ry be - yond _ our own reach. _

_____ Well, _ on a good day, _ well, I know it ain't ev-'ry day _ we _

Gtr. 1

w/Rhy. Fill 2

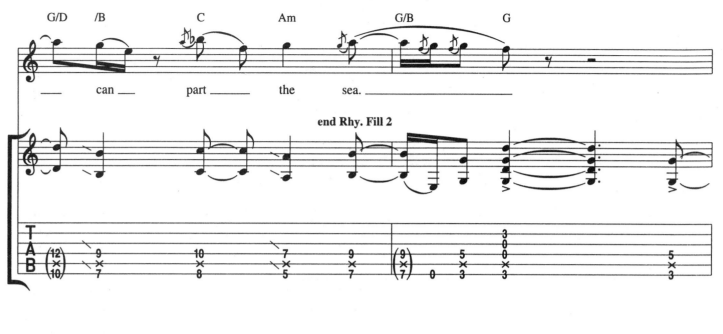

can part the sea.

end Rhy. Fill 2

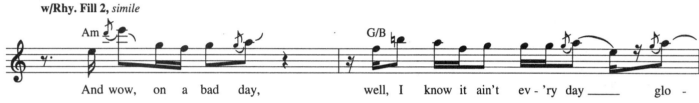

w/Rhy. Fill 2, *simile*

And wow, on a bad day, well, I know it ain't ev-'ry day ___ glo-

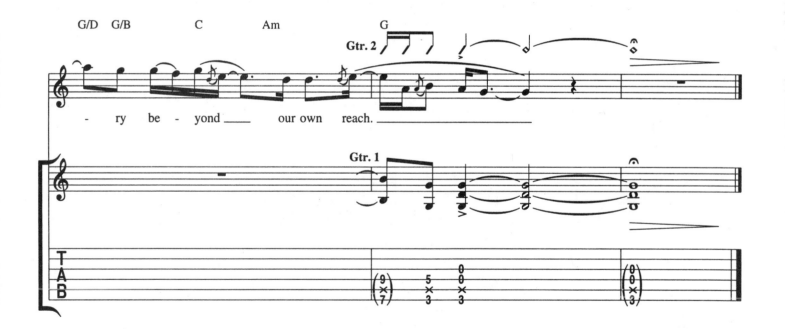

-ry be - yond ___ our own reach.

Gtr. 2

Gtr. 1

Verse 2:
You read the line every time,
Ask me about crime in my mind.
Ask me why another road song,
Funny, but I bet you never left home.

Verse 3:
Fourteen seconds until sunrise,
Tired, but wiser for the time.
Lightning thirty miles away,
Three thousand more in two days.

Wiser Time – 12 – 12

GUITAR TAB GLOSSARY **

TABLATURE EXPLANATION

READING TABLATURE: Tablature illustrates the six strings of the guitar. Notes and chords are indicated by the placement of fret numbers on a given string(s).

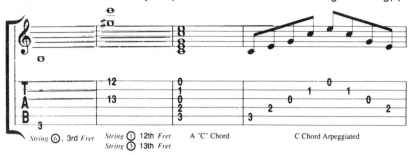

String ⑥, 3rd Fret   String ① 12th Fret   A "C" Chord   C Chord Arpeggiated
String ③ 13th Fret

BENDING NOTES

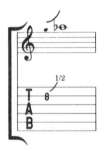

HALF STEP: Play the note and bend string one half step.*

WHOLE STEP: Play the note and bend string one whole step.

WHOLE STEP AND A HALF: Play the note and bend string a whole step and a half.

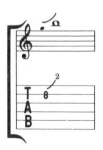

TWO STEPS: Play the note and bend string two whole steps.

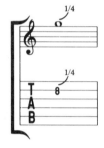

SLIGHT BEND (Microtone): Play the note and bend string slightly to the equivalent of half a fret.

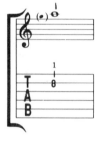

PREBEND (Ghost Bend): Bend to the specified note, before the string is picked.

PREBEND AND RELEASE: Bend the string, play it, then release to the original note.

REVERSE BEND: Play the already-bent string, then immediately drop it down to the fretted note.

BEND AND RELEASE: Play the note and gradually bend to the next pitch, then release to the original note. Only the first note is attacked.

BENDS INVOLVING MORE THAN ONE STRING: Play the note and bend string while playing an additional note (or notes) on another string(s). Upon release, relieve pressure from additional note(s), causing original note to sound alone.

BENDS INVOLVING STATIONARY NOTES: Play notes and bend lower pitch, then hold until release begins (indicated at the point where line becomes solid).

UNISON BEND: Play both notes and immediately bend the lower note to the same pitch as the higher note.

DOUBLE NOTE BEND: Play both notes and immediately bend both strings simultaneously.

*A half step is the smallest interval in Western music; it is equal to one fret. A whole step equals two frets.

© 1990 Beam Me Up Music
c/o CPP/Belwin, Inc. Miami, Florida 33014
International Copyright Secured   Made in U.S.A.   All Rights Reserved   **By Kenn Chipkin and Aaron Stang

RHYTHM SLASHES

STRUM INDICATIONS: Strum with indicated rhythm.

The chord voicings are found on the first page of the transcription underneath the song title.

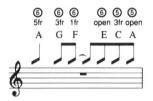

INDICATING SINGLE NOTES USING RHYTHM SLASHES: Very often single notes are incorporated into a rhythm part. The note name is indicated above the rhythm slash with a fret number and a string indication.

ARTICULATIONS

HAMMER ON: Play lower note, then "hammer on" to higher note with another finger. Only the first note is attacked.

LEFT HAND HAMMER: Hammer on the first note played on each string with the left hand.

PULL OFF: Play higher note, then "pull off" to lower note with another finger. Only the first note is attacked.

FRET-BOARD TAPPING: "Tap" onto the note indicated by + with a finger of the pick hand, then pull off to the following note held by the fret hand.

TAP SLIDE: Same as fretboard tapping, but the tapped note is slid randomly up the fretboard, then pulled off to the following note.

BEND AND TAP TECHNIQUE: Play note and bend to specified interval. While holding bend, tap onto note indicated.

LEGATO SLIDE: Play note and slide to the following note. (Only first note is attacked).

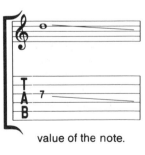

LONG GLISSAN-DO: Play note and slide in specified direction for the full value of the note.

SHORT GLISSAN-DO: Play note for its full value and slide in specified direction at the last possible moment.

PICK SLIDE: Slide the edge of the pick in specified direction across the length of the string(s).

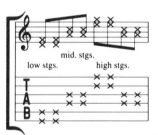

MUTED STRINGS: A percussive sound is made by laying the fret hand across all six strings while pick hand strikes specified area (low, mid, high strings).

PALM MUTE: The note or notes are muted by the palm of the pick hand by lightly touching the string(s) near the bridge.

TREMOLO PICKING: The note or notes are picked as fast as possible.

TRILL: Hammer on and pull off consecutively and as fast as possible between the original note and the grace note.

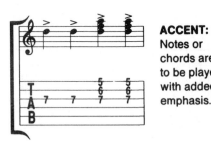

ACCENT: Notes or chords are to be played with added emphasis.

STACCATO (Detached Notes): Notes or chords are to be played roughly half their actual value and with separation.

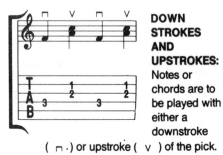

DOWN STROKES AND UPSTROKES: Notes or chords are to be played with either a downstroke (⊓) or upstroke (∨) of the pick.

VIBRATO: The pitch of a note is varied by a rapid shaking of the fret hand finger, wrist, and forearm.

HARMONICS

NATURAL HARMONIC: A finger of the fret hand lightly touches the note or notes indicated in the tab and is played by the pick hand.

ARTIFICIAL HARMONIC: The first tab number is fretted, then the pick hand produces the harmonic by using a finger to lightly touch the same string at the second tab number (in parenthesis) and is then picked by another finger.

ARTIFICIAL "PINCH" HAR-MONIC: A note is fretted as indicated by the tab, then the pick hand produces the harmonic by squeezing the pick firmly while using the tip of the index finger in the pick attack. If parenthesis are found around the fretted note, it does not sound. No parenthesis means both the fretted note and A.H. are heard simultaneously.

TREMOLO BAR

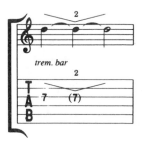

SPECIFIED INTERVAL: The pitch of a note or chord is lowered to a specified interval and then may or may not return to the original pitch. The activity of the tremolo bar is graphically represented by peaks and valleys.

UN-SPECIFIED INTERVAL: The pitch of a note or a chord is lowered to an unspecified interval.